WH
I START?

WHEN DO I START?

The Definitive Guide To Job-Hunting Success

Patrick Quinn

RIGHT WAY

Typeset in 11/12pt Times by One & A Half Graphics, Redhill, Surrey.
Printed and bound in Great Britain by Cox & Wyman Ltd., Reading,
Berkshire.

The *Right Way* series and the *Paperfronts* series are both published
by Elliot Right Way Books, Brighton Road, Lower Kingswood,
Tadworth, Surrey, KT20 6TD, U.K.

CONTENTS

To Lisa. Whom I love and admire.

Foreword

In my work as a personnel manager, I interview hundreds of people each year, for a wide spectrum of posts. These range from school-leavers hoping to become office juniors, to university graduates wishing to slot in as department heads, to highly experienced redundancy victims who will gladly take any job so long as it helps them regain their self-respect — and I am greatly in favour of that.

What strikes me, above all else, about the great proportion of candidates is their inability to *sell* themselves.

This reluctance to blow one's own trumpet is not, I am sure, a manifestation of the famous British reserve. It is, I have come to learn, nothing more than a failure to get to real grips with what they are doing. They don't realise that appropriate qualifications, immaculate turnout and nice manners are qualities shared by almost *everyone* in a given group who applies for a particular opening.

They don't see that they are one of many.

They are certainly unaware that, in order to make a potential employer sit up and take notice, they have to project an image blindingly different from that of their competitors.

For these reasons alone, I wholeheartedly recommend this book to everyone who has a desire for a better job on the one hand, and the sense of purpose to achieve it on the other.

The innovation, here, is that Patrick Quinn is convincing in his assertion that people can be marketed and promoted in the same way as soap powders, cars and cosmetics are packaged and promoted. He is believable when he says that it's not what you do, it's the way you do it which produces results. And if anybody knows how to do it, he does; because his successes in the advertising industry are a matter of record. Better still, unlike many books on the techniques of securing employment, he does it in a way that is neither patronising nor weighed down with technicalities. He is eminently readable. His style is crisp and uncluttered; his asides demonstrate genuine concern; and his ideas are strikingly creative.

If you bring as much enthusiasm to this book as Patrick Quinn so obviously has, I know it will work for you... and it will work well.

Vivienne Falla
Personnel Manager
Collection Agencies plc.

Acknowledgements

An author, any author, may believe that he is the greatest thing since the penny-farthing bike. And why not? Spending months in almost clinical isolation struggling mightily with word and phrase is not particularly conducive to modesty once the battle is on.

In reality, however, he is only a minor cog in a largish wheel. Therefore, the toughest part of writing a book is trying to find the right words to thank all those decent people who helped get it off the ground. Thus:

To Jon Donohoe for providing the cartoons and the body language illustrations. He and I have worked together for close to 25 years. And we're going to keep doing it until we get it right.

To John Powell, who thought the whole thing not a bad idea and possibly worth publishing. I defer to his judgment on the basis that he is just about the best salesman I've ever met.

To Vivienne Falla for volunteering to produce the Foreword.

And to Marion.

Thanks.

'How much to turn me into a cult figure?'

Overview

This book is written for everyone who is currently in the job market. From school-leavers and graduates searching for their first jobs; to middle-managers trapped in hierarchical dead-ends; through to highly experienced, older people floored by redundancy and stigmatised by age.

And just about everybody in between.

So whether you have a background as a college drop-out or an MA (Hons), the intention is that you'll find something of interest here.

Happily for you, since you have taken the time and trouble to lay hands on this volume, I've attempted to explore areas in the employment scheme of things which have either been glossed over or totally ignored by other authors.

Similarly, where many job-hunt books tend to major on one particular subject — on the responses to make at interviews, for instance, or on how to compose letters of application — this one throws the net far and wide and drags in a diversity of themes.

Things like:

1. Tried and tested advertising techniques that will help you sell yourself.

2. Character traits analysis; and making the most of your own attributes.

3. Job application and interview psychology.

4. Reading and using body language to your advantage at interviews.

5. How to write applications that stand right out from the crowd.

6. Devising CVs and Résumés that will get themselves read.

7. Using well-proven sales methods to sway employers' decisions.

8. Making certain that your handwriting gives the proper impression.

9. Preparing covering letters and mail-shots. Plus much more besides.

Some of these themes may not appear completely relevant at first glance. Nonetheless, there is method in this seeming madness; as I hope to prove as we progress. All I ask is that you give me a fair hearing. There could be profit in it for you.

But what gives me the divine right to set myself up as some kind of job-search guru? What qualifications do I have?

The answers to both those questions are nothing and none respectively. However, as a one-time Creative Director in the advertising business, I have hired and I have fired. Latterly, as a reasonably successful freelance in both advertising and legit writing, I have attended more interviews in which I have had to sell myself and my work to circumspect clients and publishers than you could shake a very short stick at.

As you will appreciate, in the advertising business one has to produce a new and brilliant idea every ten minutes. Yet that is the easy part. You then have to convince a third party to shell out hard-earned cash − often millions − in order to put that idea before a rightly suspicious public.

It's a case of urging the jaundiced to pay for the privilege of preaching to the indifferent.

It is not easy; but one develops a range of techniques for overcoming the myriad objections put up by people who are being urged to risk their cash and their reputations on a selling proposition that may or may not work.

Equally, as an interviewer of the famous and infamous for purposes of publication, I have become a compulsive people watcher: an observer of mannerism and dress; a diviner of fact from fiction; a differentiator between what is said and what is projected.

More pertinently, perhaps, during my thirty years in the advertising business, I've produced press, radio and television campaigns which have shifted any amount of products and services. For my money, the selling of a person and his or her abilities is no different from selling motor cars or seats on airlines.

It all comes down to the same thing − to putting up a strong selling proposition that the market will see, hear, evaluate and act upon.

To prove the point, you'll probably be aware that many of the film and TV personalities, holders of high office and business-men, one stumbles across betimes employ press agents and publicity people, whose sole function is to promote their clients' talents and bring them to the notice of a wider audience.

Let's be honest about it. Personality cults don't just happen; they are manufactured. Behind every chat-show host, pop group and, believe it, union leader, there is a publicity organisation of some kind beavering away. Again, television chat shows may appear, on the surface, to be the result of imaginative programming and offer highly popular mass entertainment. In reality, however, they are nothing short of first-rate vehicles for promoting personalities and for launching new films and books.

This being the case, it occurs to me that you, too, should have the services of a good publicity agent.

Yourself.

Further, if colourless and clay-footed politicians can have lessons in personality projection, dress sense and interview techniques, there is no good reason why you shouldn't — is there?

Well, is there?

So, certainly, I have no academic qualification which would equip me to help you find gainful employment. On the other hand, as a collator of information, and a disseminator of information, I can pass on some of the ideas and precepts of others — many of which, I am willing to bet, will cast a lot of new light on the problems of job-hunting and job-getting.

In this respect, I have called upon the talent and experience of literally hundreds of people who do have academic backgrounds relevant to our cause. People like personnel managers, behavioural psychologists, graphologists, sociologists, biologists and even the odd captain of industry or two.

Their know-how has been decanted into this book and stirred in with a soupçon of advertising and promotions know-how. The result, I believe, is a comprehensive distillation which, if put into practice, will give you a job-hunting head start over the competition.

And now a word of warning. If you find my style somewhat larky in tone, please don't assume that I view unemployment as a laughing matter. On the contrary, it is a serious cause for concern. But in my researches for the book, I discovered that personal attitude in what you write, what you say and how you conduct yourself, as you flog around the country in search of employment, is possibly the single most important aspect for success.

Thus, frame of mind is everything.

So, before we go one step farther, I urge you to put yourself into the right frame of mind for what follows. The ideas and the techniques are here for the grabbing but, just like giving up smoking or foregoing Mr Bacchus, you have to want to succeed. Not just hope to, want to; and want to more than anything else in the world.

Let me qualify that. In the past few months I have spoken to any number of unemployed people, each of whom has professed a sincere desire to find work. All of them, without exception, have compiled dozens and even hundreds of letters of application and attended numerous interviews. Significantly, the large majority viewed each rejected application as a huge disappointment, a retrograde step and a further nail in their coffin. Further discussion with them proved that they were actually expecting rejection; and they somehow found a perverse pleasure in being turned down. Only two took the opposite tack and saw every unsuccessful attempt as the result of a positive operation from which they learned something and which, given time, couldn't fail to pay dividends. As one pointed out: 'I'm getting better at this job-hunting game. I'm giving them a business proposition, telling them what I can do for them, rather than what they can do for me.'

As it turns out, both of those with the positive approach are now gainfully employed.

Oh, one more thing. You may take it as read that I am a great fan of women and believe wholeheartedly in the equality of the sexes. Even so, I should get myself into a terrible pickle if, each time I wrote the word 'he', I was forced to balance it and qualify it with the words 'or she'. It would be nonsensical. I trust that you take the point. What follows, then, despite my copious use of 'he', has no bias towards gender whatsoever — and that goes for race, colour and creed also.

Anyway, let's get on with it. Let's formulate a brief from which to work.

1.

Why They Need You
As Much As You Need Them

Scan a decent newspaper on recruitment day and you will see any number of jobs on offer. Pick up the same paper the following week and the chances are you will spot many of those vacancies still up for grabs.

Now, this is odd. Are the jobs unfilled because the advertisers failed to get the response they were looking for? Hardly. Any personnel manager will tell you that every vacancy could be filled hundreds of times over.

Why, for instance, has a national banking organisation been advertising regularly for two years for a training manager and, at the time of writing, has still not filled the post?

The answer, of course, is that the advertiser did not pick up the *quality* of response he wanted. Sure, he will have received applications from many suitably qualified people; some will possibly be over-qualified. But did he get any one reply that told him, unequivocally, that the respondent would be an asset in terms, say, of technical ability, or of profitability, or of sales improvement, or of pulling in new business?

And did this reply also go on to put substance onto these bones, not with just windy claims but with hard, provable facts?

Obviously not. Therefore, you may bet your last quid that the man or woman who ends up with the job is the one who makes a solid selling proposition.

Let's clear the decks here. Companies are in business to make profits. The people who run these companies are employed for one reason: to ensure that said profits keep rolling in. And if they can't do so with any degree of continuity, they are replaced by others who can. It therefore follows, as night follows day, that no person in such a position will risk his own livelihood by hiring staff who cannot help to give him a one-hundred per cent guarantee of success.

This, I believe, applies right across the board in every business in the land. And it applies equally to engineering, catering, electronics, building, insurance — you name it.

Many years ago a very astute businessman told me that there are only two reasons why a 'boss' employs someone. He employs him because either he can't do the job himself or won't do it. Thus, he has to pull other people into his scheme of things. In addition, it's a fact that delegating responsibility to a third party is one of the toughest decisions most people can make. 'Nobody can do it like I can do it' is a much thought, if mostly unspoken, philosophy.

So when you couple the 'can't or won't do it' types with the 'nobody does it like me' type, it becomes obvious that psychology has as much to do with job-hunting success as talent or ability. In other words, the psychology of engendering a sense of trust between the employer and the potential employee.

As an aside, it's worth mentioning that some of the most successful businessmen in history have been those who, in their early days while working for someone else, made a point of hiring people far brighter and far more able than themselves. Their policy was simple: the employee did a sterling job, but they took the credit for getting it done. They were unconcerned that the employee might usurp their own position, because nobody fires a man who consistently makes things happen. While they may have been non-productive themselves, they were worth their weight in gold to the company, merely by having the happy knack of hiring the right people.

But let's return to where we were.

I contend that even during recessionary times there are plenty of jobs about. Not as many, I'll agree, as during the good times, but still plenty. Look at it this way. People die, people retire, people are fired, people get promoted and people resign. So even when an organisation has cut its workforce to the bone, they will still require to hire staff to fill the slots when any of the above occurs.

These positions may, or may not, be advertised. This makes all the difference.

Allow me to explain. There is always an undercurrent in the job market, making it larger — far larger — than you might suppose at first glance. I am uncertain of the exact figures, but I'd make a fairly intelligent guess and say that only about 25% of all job vacancies are actually promoted in the public domain. The remaining 75%, either because the companies concerned have no advertising budget, or because they know how to locate the people they want without going into print, are never promoted.

This should, if I have laid it out properly, give you pause for thought... and encouragement.

That same newspaper, which I put into your hands a few minutes ago, may only contain fifty vacancies; but out there in limbo are a further 150 waiting to be snatched up.

And you only want one.

So, yes, companies need you as desperately as you need them. But since they have a vast marketplace from which to choose, your approach to them must be seen to be standing on its own two feet. It must work ten times as hard as the next person's. It must engender a response above and beyond the norm.

Whatever you write to them or say to them should force them to pay attention. And leave them convinced when they have.

Which leads me into a hypothesis.

Put yourself in an employer's shoes. Imagine that you have just run an ad campaign that solicits applications for, say, progamme compiler for a commercial radio station, which carries a good salary, excellent prospects and plenty of personal kudos. The response has, of course, been overwhelming and your desk, and your secretary's desk, runneth over with mail.

Assume, also, that in your advertisement you stipulated the experience and educational qualifications necessary for the job and, since the station airs only current affairs and semi-serious music programmes, you purposefully included an age-bracket which matched that of the listenership. We'll call it 30-55.

All right. How would you go about sorting through the applications so as to weed out the non-starters and come up with a shortlist? Where would you begin?

In the first place, you would almost certainly throw out the 16 to 29 and 55 to 65-year-olds. Next, you would probably dump all those very eager but inexperienced applications, followed by the ones without the necessary educational qualifications. (You understand, I hope, that we are suspending your predilection for political correctness and non-discrimination for the purposes of this example!)

This, most certainly, is the way it's done in practically every personnel office in the country. However, by using this process, could you not have dismissed out-of-hand the best 29-year-old programme compiler that broadcasting has ever seen? Maybe you did; yet you haven't got forever and you have to start somewhere. So be it.

Now for the hard bit. You will carefully sift through all remaining applications, weighing pros and cons, evaluating degrees and extent of experience. Suddenly, out of the blue, like a good deed in a naughty world, one of the applications leaps out from all the others. There, in colourful black and white it says to the effect:

I COMPILE PROGRAMMES THAT WILL BRING AUDIENCES AND ADVERTISING REVENUE THE LIKE OF WHICH HAVE NEVER BEEN SEEN BEFORE. WHAT'S MORE, I CAN PROVE IT.

I am not suggesting that these are exact words: they are simply the gist.

Now then, what would you think? You would, I submit, put this person immediately onto the shortlist, if only for entertainment value. After all, he or she is either an ego maniac, who could be the source of much amusement around the office, or a damn good programme compiler.

I am told, by people who know these things better than I do, that the great proportion of job applications are bland lists of schools attended, posts held and qualifications gained.

There is, I am assured, very little evidence of fire in the belly. A lack of get-up-and-go. A paucity of 'Look here, Charlie, can't you see that I have something outstanding to offer you?' In other words, there's no life or sparkle.

To relate this back, once again, to the advertising business (and it is very relevant, since they and you are in the selling game), no ad agency worthy of the name would ever produce a campaign that didn't make a sales proposition; that didn't make an offer or give a promise. The offer and the promise are the soul of advertising. As they also should be, I hold, in the business of job-hunting.

But I'm leaping ahead of myself. We will, a little later, go into the nuts and bolts of writing applications and framing CVs. For the moment, we should concentrate on the *attitude of mind* which will produce the kind of application that stands out and gets you noticed.

2

Take Out A Contract
On Yourself

There are two eminent physicists in the room. Both are
expounding totally opposing theories. You have never before
met either of the two, and although one is very well known to
you by name and reputation, the other is just another scientist.

You listen as they argue. You try as best you can to follow
their reasoning. Then, finally, when invited to do so, you
accept the views of one and reject the other.

Which of them did you decide to back? Don't know?

Well, let's put it this way. One is Albert Einstein and the
other isn't.

Now which one did you go with?

Albert Einstein was not only a great mathematician, he was also a pretty good self-publicist. Which is why you probably can't name any of his detractors, although many of these were equally outstanding in their field.

Right or wrong, Einstein knew that an idea was of no use unless it had an audience. But he also knew that ideas, no matter how world-shattering, could not by themselves command that audience. They had to be sold. He sold his by playing the eccentric scientist.

The oldest trick in the advertising book is this: create a need and then fill it.

You can sell your own abilities, first, by creating or demonstrating the need to the potential purchaser and, second, by going all out to satisfy the demand thus created. And you can do so in a dozen different ways.

However, there's something more you should know about Einstein. Rumour has it that he never had a bad day in his life. Contemporaries say that nothing appeared to ruffle him.

This is hard to believe of a man who had to leave his own country for fear of persecution. This is hard to believe of someone who failed the entrance examination to Zurich Polytechnic; and who was told by a schoolmaster that he would never amount to much.

The fact is, he had learned from an early age to reject negative thought and concentrate on the positive. He decided that worrying about things he couldn't, in any case, alter was a mug's game.

And so it is.

I said earlier that frame of mind is everything in the job-hunt business. I'll go farther and say that frame of mind is everything in life.

I now intend to demonstrate why.

Cast your eyes over the following statements and decide whether they relate in any particular way to your state of mind. This is not a test, merely a framework for what I wish to propose.

1. Most people who know you (family aside) would be far more concerned about leaving an umbrella in a taxi than hearing news of your sudden death.

2. Two hours after an argument with a neighbour, you are still taking time to re-run the dialogue in your mind.

3. The area in which a man lives is badly run down and the local authority has no funds with which to rectify matters. The man can either complain loudly or roll up his sleeves and start cleaning the place. He figures, however, that one man won't make much impression on the task in hand, so he continues to complain.

4. You come up with an idea, but someone shoots it down on the grounds that it has already been thought of. Consequently, you quickly forget it.

5. Yesterday the car battery ran flat. The day before, the chip-pan caught fire and the wallpaper was ruined by smoke. The day before that, the last bus was missed by five seconds, resulting in a long walk home. Why does it always happen to me?

6. Are you a 'What-iffer'? What if the interviewer doesn't like you? What if you don't pass that exam? What if you get a flat tyre? What if the sky should fall on your head?

7. What's the point of applying for that job in the paper? There will be thousands going for it.

Your reactions to the above could speak volumes about your state of mind. An examination of them should be rewarding.

1. Most of the people in the world don't know that you even exist. Most of those who do know you are rather more interested in their own affairs than yours. Each of their egos is as big, if not bigger, than yours. Which proves, if nothing else, that you should never worry about what others think of you. They generally don't care one way or the other.

Of course, this can be turned to your advantage if you adopt the correct attitude. Feeding other people's egos by concentrating on them, rather than on yourself, immediately establishes you as a 'decent type' in their minds.

Asking questions instead of making statements, and then listening carefully to the answers, is just about the best way there is to win the approval of others.

2. You may fume all you like; it won't change anything. And you can spend time dreaming up what you should have said, but you'd be far better occupied working out ways for resolving the dispute. Each minute spent on thoughts of getting even is a minute of your life completely wasted. The minutes of your life are finite. Why waste them on matters of no consequence?

3. The man must surely know that complaining will have absolutely no result. He'd be far better off making a start on the jobs himself. Even if he accomplished very little, the sense of achievement would be immense. Additionally, his efforts will almost certainly encourage others to join him (there's nothing like example to stimulate support). Then the work *will* get done.

4. I think I can say, without fear of argument, that practically everything has been done before. Most so-called new ideas are no more than variations on an old theme. So the detractor's argument is of no consequence.

Ideas are tender plants. They can be wiped out by a sneer or a shrug — usually by someone who never had an original idea in his life.

As the great writer, Oliver Wendell Holmes put it: 'There

was never an idea started that woke up men out of their stupid indifference but its originator was spoken of as a crank.'

The best course is to keep ideas out of the reach of people who have nothing to contribute but negativity. Alternatively, if some kind of critical analysis just cannot be avoided, cushion the impact by anticipating the response. Compile a list of objections beforehand — like impractical, inefficient, too expensive, illegal, and so forth — then devise a set of possible answers to these objections, or even re-work your idea to negate them. You see, even if your idea has been thought of before, there's bound to be a new hook you can swing it from.

Ideas are the lifeblood of the go-getter — even old ones.

5. Oh, woe! woe! and thrice woe! The negative thinker may believe with all his heart that he is the only one in the universe who ever has a flat battery or misses a bus, but simple observation easily proves the contrary.

The fact is, he delights in his melancholia; nothing is so pleasing to him as his sense of martyrdom. And he blows these minor annoyances up out of all proportion.

A psychologist suggests that, in chronic cases, the grief is probably unconsciously self-inflicted.

Whatever the case, if our man thinks about it, he can change his luck in a second. All he has to do is organise his life a little better than he has heretofore.

Chip-pans don't catch alight unless you put a fire under them.

6. There is a positive side to 'What-If', of course. It's part of every planning process. But What-Iffers are losers when they slip into a negative mode.

As for wanting to be accepted, you can't possibly be all things to all people — nor should you even try to be. Not everyone will agree with you or even like you; and if you worry about it you'll go to your grave still without a solution.

Worrying about what might happen is somewhat akin, if you think it through, to trying to predict the future. You are attempting to do the impossible, since crystal-gazing is hardly an exact science.

The way I see it is this.

If you expend enough effort on positively working for success, you shouldn't have the time to worry about anything unconnected with your project.

As I write this book, I have no idea at all whether it will find a publisher. However, with the benefit of past experience, plus the positive belief that what I am doing represents both a useful exercise and a saleable proposition, I am going ahead at the speed of many antelopes. I refuse to be diverted by mixed-feelings or what-ifs.

7. What's the point? What's the point of anything? Why make a cup of coffee? You only have to wash-up afterwards. Why go to the theatre? You only have to come home at the end.

'What's the point' is the last resort of the lethargic. It's one of the greatest excuses ever conceived for doing nothing. On the other hand, in the context of job-hunting, really successful people not only welcome the competition, they thrive on it.

Yes, there is a lot of competition for jobs these days. But the whole of life is a competition, isn't it? Competition is what makes the world tick; competition is what compels humanity to produce increasingly better ideas.

To compete is to fight — with propositions that pull no punches and mince no words, with concepts that come out shooting, with a self-belief that doesn't duck, weave or feint, but plants the right-hook square on the opposition's chin.

Consider this. If you win a job in the face of competition from several thousand other hopefuls, just think how very special that makes you.

In any case, someone has to get it, so it might as well be you.

The moral of all this is to be positive — especially about yourself. Bear in mind that you are, without fear or favour, unique. There is nobody else in the world quite like you. Nobody has the same compilation of knowledge; nobody has the same breadth of skills; nobody has the same logical processes, range of emotions, sense of humour.

You are, sir or madam, exceptional. Like your fingerprints, you are unparalleled.

You may care to know that it is every advertising copywriter's dream to work on a product which is totally and unequivocally unique. Such products are, in the general run of things, rarer than cabs on a wet night.

Yet, here we are, eyeball to eyeball with just such a product. *You.*

Surely, we can package, promote and market a product that is so quintessentially different — not to mention useful, adaptable, creative, flexible, motivated and skilful?

Yes, we can. And we shall. Because on the grounds of recognising your uniqueness, you are already making the decision to expunge negative thought and allow the positive to take over.

You can, if you wish, go one step farther and put this decision in writing.

On the following page is a Contract of Attitude that I hope you will negotiate with youself. I ask you to read it and sign it, photocopy it and put it in your wallet or handbag. It will be a good practice if you refer to it from time to time, particularly when you catch yourself in the throes of negative thought. Remember, too, that a contract is binding upon both parties and renegers are likely to incur swingeing action from the party of the second part.

Banal? Puerile? Beneath your dignity? Well, you can see it that way if you care to; and you can accept and ignore it as the whim takes you. It is, after all, no more than a knot-in-a-handkerchief reminder. It could, however, be the start of something big.

Go on, give it a whirl. You may be surprised how positive it will make you feel.

CONTRACT OF ATTITUDE

I, ... Enter into binding Contract and Resolve herewith to dismiss all Negative Attitude from my life. Henceforth I shall not:

1. *Attempt to change things I cannot change.*
2. *Go out of my way to 'get even'.*
3. *Worry about events which might occur.*
4. *Rummage through past mistakes.*
5. *Let others' comments condition me.*
6. *Be a 'hard-done-by' victim.*

Conversely, henceforth I shall:

1. *Be positive in every respect.*
2. *Make the most of my attributes.*
3. *Take setbacks in my stride.*

Signed . . . .

Dated this . . . . . day of . . . . 19. . . . .

3.

What Kind Of Person
Are You?

Thus far, we have formulated half our working brief. We know we've got a pretty remarkable product on our hands; but we have to figure out its Unique Selling Proposition. That is, the single attribute which sets it aside from, and makes it better than, anything the competition can offer.

Following normal advertising agency practice, I think we can do this by assessing exactly what kind of person you are. Where do we find your on-switch? How do you operate? Are you a thinker or a doer? Are you a creative type or an implementer?

Below is a list of words and phrases, any number of which may describe the sort of person you are. Browse through the list, and when you come across a word or phrase that seems to fit your image of yourself, give it a tick. You can tick as few or as many as you wish, but do try to be honest with yourself. Also, ignore the prefix letters and numbers for the moment; and please don't sneak a look at the Analysis Chart until you've fully completed the list.

Ready?

WHO ARE YOU?

CHARACTER APPRAISAL

Are you:

(1) Unconventional?
(a) Placid?
(a) Dependable?
(a) Tolerant?
(a) Logical?
(1) A chance taker?
(a) Thorough?
(1) Undisciplined?
(1) Argumentative?
(a) Slow to anger?

(1) Flexible?
(a) Conventional?
(1) Easily roused?
(1) Intuitive?
(a) Inflexible?
(1) Judgmental?
(a) Uncritical?
(a) Practical?
(1) Restless?
(1) Disorganised?

PHYSICAL & INTELLECTUAL ANALYSIS

Do you:

(a) Enjoy sports and pastimes that depend on methodical skills? (Model-making, playing an instrument, d.i.y., golf.)

(1) Enjoy sports and pastimes which depend mainly upon physical effort? (Football, tennis, dancing, karate.)

(1) Play word-games or devise film-plots in your head?

(a) Need all the facts at your fingertips before coming to a decision?

WHO ARE YOU? (contd.)

(1) Rarely read the instructions before starting a self-assembly kit?

(a) Number or somehow mark the parts of a mechanism you have taken apart?

(1) Put off until tomorrow what you don't feel like doing today?

(a) Ensure that necessary jobs are done as soon as possible?

COMMUNICATIONS APPRAISAL

Are you:

(1) The one in a group who makes the decision about what to do or where to go?

(a) A good listener in whom people confide?

(a) Precise in your instructions to others?

(1) A good talker, with plenty of anecdotes and stories?

(1) Prepared to argue vigorously to have your ideas accepted?

(a) Irritable with people who fail to follow your instructions to the letter?

(1) The life and soul of the party?

(a) Reluctant to speak in strange company?

(a) Uncomfortable with people who misuse words or employ bad grammar?

(1) Easily encouraged to talk about yourself?

(a) The soul of discretion?

(1) Quick to criticise?

WHO ARE YOU? (contd.)

DRESS ANALYSIS

Do you dress:

(1) To attract attention   (a) Very conventionally?
    to yourself?

(a) To win approval?   (1) In order to shock?

(a) For the occasion?   (1) Fashionably?

(1) Casually?   (a) Soberly?

All right, as you've no doubt guessed, the (1) prefixes represent the creative end of the spectrum, while the (a) prefixes are the characteristics found in administrators and organisers.

Therefore, if you ticked more (a) prefixes than (1) prefixes, you are inclined towards the conservative. And vice-versa. If you scored an abundance of (a) prefixes, you are a supervisory type who enjoys method and order. While a plentitude of (1)s suggests you are rather more a seat-of-the-pants, adrenalin-driven creator. The former dislike loose ends and find intuitive work difficult. The latter thrive on disorder and despise committees and paperwork.

Both types, however, are invaluable.

There would be no new products without the creator; and there would be no organisation for selling those products without the sales manager.

Anyway, although the check-list hasn't told you anything you didn't already know, at least it's now down in black and white. It gives you a springboard to launch yourself from.

The object of this exercise, it should be pointed out, is not to highlight character/intellectual/communication and dress faults, or suggest that you should expunge those traits which don't conform to some magic formula that I have concealed up my sleeve. On the contrary, the purpose is to define exactly the type you are so that you can market yourself to the full. Self-knowledge is probably the single most important weapon in the armoury for winning people over to your team — which is exactly what you have to achieve in any job-hunt situation.

In any event, it would be nigh on impossible to change a character, with all its facets and convolutions, that you have been living with for decades. On the other hand, it's the simplest thing in the world to tailor *attitude*. And, when you think about it, no matter how outrageous you may be in dress or speech, it's your attitude to others that convinces them whether or not you are a decent person to be acquainted with.

Look at it this way. You may be number 250 on the manager's interview list. You may be too young or too old for the job. You may even be under-qualified or under-experienced for the job in question. But if your attitude is right, you could go straight onto the short-list. The right attitude will wipe out the drawbacks of numbers, age and experience as effectively as a well-aimed Kalashnikov.

What I ask you to do, right now, is look back over the check-list and write out on a separate sheet those traits and characteristics you have ticked. Now, immediately beneath each of these headings, jot down a few words explaining what the particular characteristic means to you; then, on another line, illustrate how each trait may be moulded into a *benefit* for a potential employer.

Maybe I should explain.

We'll say that your list contains the following. (I've chosen only four — for brevity's sake.)

Dependable.

Enjoy physical sports.

A good listener.

A fashionable dresser.

Given the fact that you seriously believe these are a true representation of yourself (and I mean seriously), you might write the following:

Dependable

I'm punctual. I'd rather be twenty minutes early than three minutes late. In addition, I dislike letting people down.

Benefit: *An employer can rely on me to get the job done on time. I'd probably be good at Production Management, Publishing or working in a Print Costing and Estimating department.*

Enjoy Physical Sports

I like the buzz that hard exercise gives me — not to mention the sense of comradeship with other players.

Benefit: *I'm competitive; and all business is competitive. I can also operate easily as part of a team. This means I could fit into a job where teamwork is essential — Advertising, the Hotel trade or Catering, and Sales Promotion.*

A Good Listener

People like to talk to me. They tell me their problems and the latest gossip; and I can keep a secret.

Benefit: *An employer can rely on my tact and discretion to deal with customers direct; indicating Sales, Secretarial, or Customer Relations. And what about Personnel Management?*

A Fashionable Dresser

I feel good when I'm well-dressed. To me, being well-dressed means being in fashion.

Benefit: *An employer could unhesitatingly use me in any situation where meeting the public face-to-face is an important part of his business. Retail Sales. Reception work. Leisure Industry.*

A word of caution. None of the above is meant to propose that you must suddenly up and change an occupation for which you may have trained and worked over any number of years. These are merely my interpretations, since I have no idea of your abilities and skills. What it should do, however, is show you the way to turn personal characteristics into saleable, and therefore readily buyable, commodities, whether you intend to stick to your chosen trade or whether you intend to diversify. Because the words you write beneath each benefit heading will be concise manifestations of your attitude to work.

As we said earlier: attitude is everything.

There is the story of a man, probably apocryphal, who was so frightened of dying that... he shot himself. How about that for attitude?

On the other hand, I can relate a true tale of a friend of mine. He was terrified of flying; all the symptoms of fear, the sweaty palms and butterflies, manifested themselves whenever he made a plane journey. Fortunately, his trips by air were rare, but then a job promotion came along which demanded that he take frequent flights abroad. The prospect worried him greatly. It was a case of either putting up with the fear or resigning from a highly-paid job.

As it turns out, he did neither. He examined his attitude and decided on a new motivation. He went along to a flying club, where he took lessons. Within three months he had gained a Private Pilot's Licence. Now he understands the risks, and he realises that blind, ignorant fear had not only framed his attitude, but also nearly robbed him of his livelihood.

For the record, you will be employing the *benefits* you have written down, after suitable paring and editing, for inclusion in letters of application and CVs. These topics will come up in later chapters.

In the meantime, let's forget about us and talk about other people. Or, rather, let's talk about our interest in other people. It's important, I assure you.

4.

Make Capital
From The Interest

You may think you are the centre of the universe, but you can take it from me that, in the eyes of others, you aren't. They are. People may like you, but they like themselves much more. Indeed, nothing is more important to them than themselves. This is a sweeping generalisation, and I concede that there may be one or two who, as a habit, think more of others than of themselves, but it is for all intents and purposes true.

Take names, for instance. I can assume with a fair degree of certainty, that my name ignites no deep feelings within your breast. Likewise, unless you are called Bo Derek or Michelle Pfeiffer, yours would not mean much to me. Yet, to each of us without exception, our name is immensely significant. Every Robert, Sally, Jack and Jill of us is over the moon with his or her own identity.

The best salespeople know the value of this phenomenon.

Their sales pitches start with the prospect's name, are discreetly interspersed with the prospect's name, and end with the prospect's name. If they are really clever, they also drop the prospect's wife's name somewhere in the proceedings, along with those of the kids, and the cat, the dog and the budgie for good measure.

But this pathological concern by the population at large with 'self' is good. Once you grasp the simple truth of it, you can turn it to your advantage.

A very famous American advertising copywriter, who worked for a huge department store, was once reprimanded by his Chairman for writing too much copy in an advertisement for the store. The Chairman, whom we'll call Tom Jackson, told the writer that nobody would bother to read so much verbiage. The writer disagreed. 'Tell you what,' he said. 'I bet I could write a full page ad, crammed with words, and you would read every single bit of it.'

Tom Jackson took the bet. 'Do it,' he ordered, 'and I'll prove you wrong.'

'Well, sir,' the writer responded, 'I don't have to. I'll just tell you the headline.'

'Go ahead.'

'The headline says: This advertisement is all about Tom Jackson.'

That writer knew the importance of identity.

Everyone, even the dyed-in-the-wool introvert, has a measure of self-esteem. Most people, whether they show it or not, enjoy having the attention of others. Nay, they crave it. Just listen to any conversation in any pub and you'll hear egos being exercised: 'I think... I reckon... I know... I'm sure'. It's a manifestation of the glorious, self-centred 'I' swaggering from table to table, to bar, and back again.

Keep your eyes on these conversations. Invariably there will be a constant listener — someone who nods, smiles, asks a question or two, and then waits attentively for the, usually, long-winded answer. Were you able to ask the 'talker' what he thought of the 'listener', you would probably get an answer along the lines of: 'He's a great bloke — terrific conversationalist.'

A great bloke? A terrific conversationalist? No — he's a super salesman of a product called *interest*. The profit on his sales comes in many forms. He is accepted, he is liked, he is considered a good guy to have around. But the most important aspect comes in the shape of his ability to influence the other person. He is in a position to get his own way, and the other fellow will think it's his own idea.

I believe it goes without saying that any interest you show in others must be a genuine interest. There is nothing more obviously counterfeit than a feigned interest. Those cocktail party questions, asked simply for the sake of conversation, put an abrupt end to any potential relationship; especially when the interrogator's attention is obviously elsewhere while the answer is being given.

We've all been there, haven't we? 'Hi — I'm Roland Butter. Our hostess tells me you're a pilot. What do you fly?'

'Well, I'm checked out on Cessna 152s, Bulldogs and Cherokees; and I have a twin-rating...'

At which point, you see Mr Butter's eyes swivelling towards the long-legged blonde in the corner, and for all the difference it would make you could be reciting the telephone directory A to K. Old Roland, you see, is only waiting for you to finish so that he can tell you what *he* flies... and at great length, too. If you have any sense, of course, you will listen attentively; he might make a good ally.

A better plan would have been to turn the question back on him right at the start, with something like: 'Yes, I am. Do *you* fly?'

Is this mercenary? Yes, it is. But it's only by way of illustration; and the moral is that when you give someone your attention, give them all of it.

A good friend of mine, who also happens to run a multi-million pound business, has a philosophy about interest: 'When I hire people, I look for two things. One: does this fellow just want a job, any job, or is he interested in my objectives? Two: has he done his homework?

'In the first case, I'm often appalled by the number of people who want *me* to do something for them, rather than suggest that *they* could do something for me. One fellow recently, I swear, told me that my company could be good for his career. And he wondered why I cut the interview short.

'In the second case, I find that some really well-qualified, highly intelligent people have not bothered to do even basic research on our products, services and customers. It's so easy to do: a phone call to our receptionist will produce a copy of our Annual Report, plus a whole sheaf of leaflets and brochures detailing our products and services. Take a trip to the public library, to unearth the relevant 'blue book' — the directory of our industry — and you'll find the names of our directors, the names and locations of subsidiary companies, and details of who owns whom. Finally, a visit to Companies House will allow you to get a look at our accounts in detail. Simple.

'Yet it seems like too much trouble. So to come across someone who is familiar with the company, its turnover and its products is like hearing your number called in a raffle.

'If they show no interest in me, other than that I can supply a wage packet, how can I be interested in them?'

Echo answers: how?

On a slightly different tack, dealing with attitude rather more than interest, another businessman of my acquaintance says this:

'My company uses a lot of manpower. We recruit on a regular basis. By the nature of things, we see great numbers of unemployed people. Being unemployed is no disgrace; and just because a man is on the dole it doesn't follow, by any means, that he is unemployable. But it's what he does while he's on the dole that engages me... greatly.

'Let's say I have two applicants, both unemployed. During the interview it turns out that man or woman A has no hobbies, no pursuits to keep the mind occupied, and spends most of the time (apart from writing letters of application for jobs) watching television.

'On the other hand, applicant B has worked on the garden, built a shed, decorated the house, done odd jobs for pensioners... perhaps he's five chapters into writing a book... whatever.

'Which of these do I take on? It's obvious. I take the bloke with a bit of backbone; the one who refuses to roll over.

'Nonetheless, I see dozens of the former; and they can't understand why I absolutely won't bother to use their services.

'I realise, obviously, that chap B could be making it all up. But even this shows that he has prepared himself. He is displaying an interest in winning me over.'

Businesses are in business to do more business — there is no other reason for their existence. Thus, you can be qualified to the hilt with every diploma known to academia, but if your application or your personal demeanour neglects to demonstrate an abiding interest in the company — meaning an interest in the interviewer and his or her problems insofar as filling the position are concerned — then you are doomed to failure.

My investigations make it very plain. Most people who hire and fire are only human. They need approbation just as readily as you do. They need to be seen to be on top of their job, working for the good of the company, producing new employees who won't let the side down. In this respect, they are as vulnerable as the next person to the right attitude... to genuine attention. The way to hit a person's sweet-spot is to talk to him about the one thing that interests him above all others.

Consider this, too. The man who interviews you may very well appear to be on top of everything and highly successful... king of the hill. But what you must realise is that he has his problems, also. His wife may despise him and treat him like a dish-rag; his children could be in detention centres; and he may, that very morning, have picked up a speeding ticket which will wipe out his driving licence.

Remember these things as you address him, either on paper or in person; and treat him the way you, with all your worries and concerns, would wish to be treated.

Here are five points to remember in the interest stakes:

1. Interviewers like their names to be mentioned during conversation, and regularly. It's unwise, however, to employ the person's Christian name unless invited to do so.

2. They want their egos massaged, with questions that illustrate how important their jobs are. Like: 'You mean you're the Personnel Manager for the *whole* plant?'

3. They know what they're looking for, so do your homework and make sure they get it. Show interest in the company.

4. They make decisions upon which the future of the company may depend. Convince them that you can contribute to that future.

5. Above all, they need to hire people who, by word and deed, will help the company towards greater profitability. This will reflect on them and make them look good. And looking good is their life's work!

You can't win an argument

People who hire and fire, by the very nature of their job, will often set traps for an interviewee to fall into. The object of this exercise is to gauge your measure of diplomacy, discretion and tact; because if they are going to let you loose on their customers, or on the rest of their workforce, they will want to know whether you are going to start a fight every time someone says something with which you disagree.

For instance, they will make a patently contentious statement and then sit back and await the response. The best way to illustrate this, I think, is to relate a factual experience.

When I was a good deal younger, and a good deal brasher than I am now, I attended a series of interviews for a sales job with a multi-national company which manufactured a range of popular consumables. The first interview went swimmingly, but the second appointment, a few days later, was conducted by two executives who, it seemed to me, were 'out to get me'. The questions came thick and fast and I barely had time to consider my responses.

Finally, one of the interviewers took a copy of the company's four-colour product brochure out of a drawer and handed it to me. 'This was printed silk-screen,' he said off-handedly.

Now, at that point in my life, I had had a number of years in the printing trade; and if there was one thing this brochure definitely wasn't it was silk-screen processed. And I said so, in no uncertain terms. An argument developed, with the interviewer defending his position as tenaciously as I was.

Realising that we were getting nowhere, I capitulated, saying that he could be right — but not believing it for a moment. It was, however, too late. The interviewer had been aware of my printing background and had deliberately set me up.

Not completely unexpectedly, the job went to someone else. To somebody, no doubt, who wasn't so quick off the mark to demonstrate how knowledgeable he was but, more importantly, to someone who knew that the only way to win an argument is to avoid it.

By attempting to put the interviewer straight, even though he was playing me like a fish, I was going out of my way to make him feel inferior. How unutterably stupid.

Even so, the lesson was learned. In forty years of working for a living, and with many interviews attended, that was practically the only job I failed to get.

We'll talk at length, later on, about the tricks that interviewers employ in order to plumb the depths of your character.

5.

How Interviewers Work

Ralph Palmen is a highly successful lecturer on business matters; his Palmen Institute is known all over the United States as a criterion of business training. In an article in *Sales & Marketing Update,* he spoke to business managers about the secrets of successfully hiring the right people.

I now reproduce the essence of his remarks, on the premise that he lays ground-rules which show us *how* an interviewer makes his mind up and *why* he chooses one person rather than another. So if we know what the interviewer is thinking, we can give him what he wants.

This is what Ralph Palmen wrote:

'Have you ever hired an employee and, 30 days later, wondered why? Learning to hire the right employee is one of the most difficult, and the most important, skills any manager learns. By learning a few principles, and practising them regularly, you will experience fewer management problems and higher levels of productivity.

One: The next time you have a job to fill, ask yourself the following questions:

(a) What are the specific results I want to accomplish through this person's efforts?

(b) What are the skills needed to get the job done?

(c) What single most important skill is needed to achieve these results?

(d) What do I have to offer someone in exchange for their accomplishments?

(e) What type of person tends to be most successful working for me?

Two: Be a creative recruiter.
Advertise for qualities rather than experience.

Three: Prepare for the interview.
Before you interview, write down the questions you intend to ask. Ask everyone the same questions. And always remember: listen a lot, and say as little as possible.

Four: Think twice about hiring the over-qualified.
When you hire someone who is over-qualified for the position, you are hiring a person who has no room to grow in his or her job. They are hard to motivate.

Five: Check references.
You check references to verify your opinions. Ask open-ended questions of referees, get them to tell you what this person needs in the way of management or help to achieve his potential in life.

Six: Let candidates know what you have decided, but don't tell them why.
In most cases, telling people why you did not hire them does them no good.'

That's the bones of Ralph Palmen's piece. What can we make of it? How can we turn this knowledge to our advantage? Let's take the points in order.

One:
We know that the interviewer is looking for a specific result from our employment. He knows the skills required to do the job, and he has an idea of the type of applicant who fits into his particular firm.

For our part, we have identified that we can tackle the work from the job-description in his ads. Through judicious questioning and by evaluating the kind of man he is — by seeing how he dresses, by observing his body-language and, above all, by listening to his view of the world in general, we can slot into his notional frame of reference for the perfect employee.

Two:
The experience aspect of the job should be cut and dried. If it isn't, he will probably be offering training. In this latter case, he is hunting for the kind of person who learns quickly, who can be motivated, or who will act upon his own initiative.

It isn't too hard, by demonstrating past learning achievements (you have half-a-dozen GCSEs, or you took German/Woodwork/Computer studies at evening class, or you have a degree or business management qualification), to prove both aptitude and motivation.

Three:
If the interviewer has a set-piece questionnaire then, depending on the type of job he is offering and with your knowledge of that job, you can predict with a fair degree of accuracy the questions he will put. Just put yourself in his shoes. What questions would you pose?

Four:
This illustrates clearly enough the futility of chasing a job for which one is over-qualified. Taking on employment which is beneath your abilities is not destined to last very long. On the other hand, where employment is imperative and is an end in itself, there is a good case for understating your experience and achievements.

Five:
When you offer the names of acquaintances and past employers as referees, be absolutely sure that, when the time comes, they will do you justice. Can there be anything worse than a lack-lustre reference? I doubt it. All references are, or should be, positive. But some are a good deal more positive than others.

Six:
You've been waiting days for a decision. It finally comes in the shape of a three-line letter that says to the effect, sorry, chum, you didn't get it. Don't take this numbing brevity as being any reflection upon your performance at the interview. The letter is as bland as it is to disarm the litigious. It's well documented that some employers who have given reasons to candidates for their decision not to hire, have found themselves in court for their pains!

6.

If It Don't Quack, It Ain't A Duck!

Have you ever noticed that the most successful people are those who seem to be the luckiest? Not only are they in very desirable positions, they also get all the breaks. If they fell backwards into the proverbial mire, they'd come up smelling of violets.

Makes you sick, doesn't it?

But, think about it, this is no accident. In the first place, there is no such thing as luck — only opportunity. In the second place, those who always fall on their feet *make* their opportunities.

Being in the right place at the right time has nothing to do with chance and is not dependent upon some benevolent fairy godmother. Being in the right place at the right time means going out of your way to make the journey towards opportunity; and if you make enough journeys, by the law of probabilities something is bound to pay off sometime.

The point is, we never find out how many disappointing

excursions the successful make. Go-getters keep their failures strictly to themselves — they think them not worth thinking about, let alone talking about. So we observe in them only that quality we like to define as luck.

Conversely, the failures amongst us never stop talking about their rotten luck. Usually, they undertake a given project with much verbal fanfare and trumpeting. When it doesn't work, which of course it doesn't, they never stop bemoaning the fact. Which leads me, right now, to invent an old Chinese proverb. 'He who puts only one iron in fire will not set world alight.'

I have said all this for a reason.

In the advertising business, there is a selling device called Direct Mail. You will not only have heard of it, but will also have received it — and possibly by the cartload — from companies trying to sell you everything from a magazine subscription to a time-share apartment on the Costa del Sol.

Now, however cheesed off you and thousands of others may become at all this unwanted material decanting through your letter-box, there is one simple and incontrovertible fact you should bear in mind: direct mail works. It works because it spreads its message like a trawl net throughout the carefully chosen marketplace. Lots of minnows may very well fall through the holes, but the catch of healthy haddock makes the whole business very worthwhile.

It follows, I think, that anyone in the job market would be a mug if he were not in the direct mail business. In other words, if he were not producing and mailing a trawl-net letter aimed at every potential employer in the Yellow Pages.

What? You say you've already done so? Not like this, you haven't.

Your Job Club is overflowing with examples of begging letters? Not like this, it isn't.

A mail-shot should open with a bang and close with a flourish. It should be short, sharp and straight to the point. It should not beat around the bush, be timid or coy, or hide lights under bushels. And it should not, decidedly not, beg anyone's pardon for being in existence. In short, it should hit the reader straight between the eyes and leave him wanting more.

In approaching a potential employer via a mail-shot, you can afford to adopt a confident approach. You have something valuable to sell; and you have absolutely nothing to lose, save a second-class stamp, if the prospect fails to bite. Even so, the piece itself must have a respectable feel to it. What I mean by this is that it should be neatly typed on good quality *white* paper, with the full name and address of the recipient in evidence, with his or her name in the opening salutation, and delivered in a crisp, *white* envelope. A white envelope, by definition, is not a 'business circular' envelope and has a far greater chance of being opened, as opposed to finding itself dumped, unread, into the waste bucket. There is a school of thought which says that letters of this kind should arrive unfolded, in white, card-backed A4 envelopes. If you can afford the cost of the stationery, I'm in favour of it. Is there anything more agreeable than receiving a pristine, uncreased, fresh off the press communication? I think not. And it shows that you care.

Presentation is therefore most important. Content is just as significant. Perhaps we should see what I mean. The first mailer example might be written by someone with very little work experience. The second is by somebody well qualified.

This first letter demonstrates a number of interesting things.

1. You are *ambitious*.

2. You have done your *homework* on the company.

3. You have foreseen Mr Rich's *needs*.

4. You have *imagination*.

5. You are offering Mr Rich a sales *proposition*.

6. You exhibit good *business sense*.

7. You are *confident* in yourself.

8. Above all, you have shown *interest*.

(Mail-Shot 1.)

Roland Butter
24 Letsbee Avenue · Staines
Middlesex · ST1 0H4
Telephone: 0434 071428

Robin D. Rich, Esq.
Personnel Director
Consolidated Clocks Limited
Tempus Fugit Works
Retford
Nottinghamshire NS7 4DW

24th August (Year)

Dear Mr Rich,

Would you stake your reputation on somebody who doesn't
have one? Fortunately, I'm not asking you to. What I would
ask, however, is the opportunity to prove that I could become
a valuable member of your organisation.

Aged 20, I have only modest work experience. Even so, I do
have three GCSEs, plus a Duke of Edinburgh Silver Award,
and am currently taking a nightschool Sales Training Course.

I am aware that your company has recently launched a
number of new products – the Dingbat Digital and the
Hourglass Alarm, among others. Consequently, you may be
thinking of recruiting for your Sales Team.

I should be obliged, therefore, if you would be kind enough to
consider me for any potential position. Better still, I would
welcome a personal interview.

Should you care to know more, or see more, please do get in
touch.

Most sincerely,

Roland Butter

All of which qualities are welcomed by business people. But most especially the display of genuine interest in the company, its products and future. As we said earlier, when you show real, knowledgeable interest in another person, you are massaging them right where they like it.

Of course, there's nothing hard and fast about this letter. The whole thing can be adapted to suit any given company, while the line about new products can be adjusted for, say, a supermarket chain currently building a new branch:

'I am aware that your company is soon to open a new, 200,000 square feet branch in Colchester. Consequently, you may be thinking of recruiting trainee management staff...'

Or for an architect's office which has won a large contract:

'I am aware that your company has been awarded the design and site management contract for the new leisure complex in Bristol. Consequently, you may be thinking of recruiting administrative personnel...'

Most large companies issue press releases when they are launching major projects. Thus, the information you need for this part of the spiel can be gleaned from local newspapers and regional television reports. Another method is to keep your eyes open for the hoardings erected by builders around new commercial developments. Invariably, there's a sign of some kind which indicates exactly what is going on.

Does it seem like too much work to edit every single mailer? The real question is: do you have anything better to do? Also: how badly do you need a job?

In the second mailer, you say it like it is. You major on your achievements in highly colourful black and white. You neither pull punches nor employ modesty − false or otherwise. And, obviously, you tailor the message to suit the nature of the job and your own attributes.

The main thrust of the piece, however, is the offer to show a given company how to improve its sales figures (or its production output, or its packaging process, or whatever your line happens to be). Such an offer, if stated sincerely with confidence, is practically unrejectable. Any sales director

(Mail-Shot 2.)

**Aaron A. G. String
17 Highwayman Close
Andover
Hampshire AN3 5ES
Telephone: 0909 223301**

Mr C. D. Cake,
Sales Director
Castle Plastics
Edinburgh EH45 8VW

8th May (Year)

Dear Mr Cake,

Would you care to discover how to increase your sales of domestic rainware and sub-surface products by at least 30% in the next twelve months?

As Regional Sales Manager for a polymer manufacturer, I increased sales by 43% in just eighteen months.

And what I can do for them, I can do for you.

Thus, if you need a Sales Manager with real ability, perhaps you may be interested in knowing a little more.

The 43% sales increase was achieved by:

(1) Developing existing accounts and introducing new customers.

(2) Launching customer promotions and discount packages. (These were later adopted nationally.)

(3) Implementing an innovative sales-training programme.

Not to put too fine a point on it, I have exceeded sales targets every year of my career.

I have a good chemistry degree and am married with a grown-up family.

To find out more − all you have to do is ask. I will be more than pleased to enlarge upon the foregoing at any interview you may care to grant.

Yours sincerely,

Aaron String

worth the name will know that a brief chat loses nothing, but could gain a lot.

IMPORTANT NOTE

Both mailers are, of course, off-the-cuff and impromptu submissions. Each could, however, be tailored somewhat to act as decent Covering Letters when you are sending a CV to a prospective employer in response to an ad. And remember, never, ever, send a CV *without* a covering letter. It is the height of rudeness and will count against you.

In any case, the secret of both mailers lies in their brevity. They say a good deal in very few words. And if you are enclosing a CV for either, then say so at the end of each mailer, along the following lines:

I am pleased to enclose my Curriculum Vitae for your consideration.

If you take the trouble to look at advertising copy in magazines or the daily press, you will see just how powerful a few words can be. The very best of ad copy is a work of art and a real labour of love − with the emphasis on labour. A dozen lines may take hours, even days, to prepare; with each word weighed for effect and emphasis. You should strive for the same kind of effect and emphasis in your mailers.

There is a technique for creating pithy writing of this kind.

First, write the piece as usual.

Second, go through it and delete all extraneous words and phrases. Be tough on yourself, and leave nothing that doesn't add some substance to the thrust of your message.

Third, put it away in a drawer and forget it for a day or two.

Fourth, get it out and read it from the point of view of the recipient. Does it still have the original punch? Or is it just bland, without life or sparkle.

Fifth, if it's the former, put it straight into the post.

Sixth, if the latter, either re-write completely, or go through it again — editing and dumping all the dross.

Very few people are able to produce a powerful mailer at the first draft. Like everything worthwhile in this life, you get out only what you put in.

IMPORTANT NOTE
Selective Information Means You Cannot
Be Ruled Out

You put into a mailer only what is *necessary*. It doesn't contain the same in-depth information to be found in a Curriculum Vitae. Therefore, you cannot be rejected on the grounds of not, for instance, holding some particular qualification, or of being currently unemployed, or such-like.

In these circumstances, the only way you can be rejected is because there is no position available or imminent.

As an aside, you may be tempted to ask a third party to give an opinion of your letter. I'd advise you to be somewhat circumspect about doing so, unless you tell them the precise psychology behind it — or have them read this book. Otherwise their reaction is very likely to be a negative one. Without a complete understanding of the motivational strategy, other people's opinions are certain to be subjective and therefore of little value.

To reinforce this: if Thomas Alva Edison had listened to others when they called him a dreamer and a crank, he wouldn't have gone on to patent more than 1,000 inventions — including the light bulb, the phonograph and motion-picture equipment.

My advice is to go with your own instincts; because success

in most things is determined by what your bones tell you to be right. As they say, Faint-heart never won Fair Lady.

I am reminded of an aspiring copywriter who had made many overtures for employment to a particular advertising agency — all to no effect. Then, one day, he discovered that the firm was working on a campaign for a drug abuse agency. He wrote a short note to the creative director, including in the envelope a small polythene bag containing a white substance (talcum powder, as it turned out).

The note, which also detailed his name and address, said simply.

DRUGS ARE FOR MUGS!

He was working for the company the following week.

It's this ability to produce a supplication that stands out from the mass of other material that wins the day.

Worth remembering, too, is the fact that very few people become successes overnight; and even the famous have continually to consolidate their positions. The stories of well-known film actors and actresses, for instance, who still have to beg producers in order to secure a given role, are a matter of common knowledge. Life is a competition; and to compete is to fight. This means that if you don't have the stomach for it or, more correctly, are embarrassed about putting yourself out on a limb, or are frightened of rejection, you will quickly be by-passed by those who aren't.

So you've got to make your message stick. It has to mean what it says, and say what it means. Because if it doesn't quack, it ain't a duck — and if it doesn't sell, it won't work.

A quick extra word about presentation. If you don't have a personal letterhead, you may be wise to get some printed. Those high-street prompt print outfits will do a first-class job; and the impression that well-designed letterheads have upon prospects is well worth the outlay. I leave you to decide whether to enclose a stamped, addressed envelope for a reply. I know that many companies don't bother to reply even when an s.a.e. is included. Yes, good manners dictates that you should get a response; but mailing costs money and, sometimes, a company might have to reply to thousands of letters. Ask yourself a question. Do you reply in writing to every piece of mail that comes through your letterbox — including the advertising and promotional literature? Of course not.

I guess the psychology of it is that when you fail to get a reply, you somehow suppose that your submission has not been seen and you are being ignored. This is unlikely to be the case. So be a bit philosophical about it.

Anyway, it stands to reason that you'll get a higher percentage of response with an s.a.e. enclosed than without.

IMPORTANT NOTE

When you sit down to write to a prospective employer — either via a mailer or a full-blown CV — bear in mind the *features and benefits* of your own character and abilities we worked out in Chapter 3. Then, where it's feasible, work them into the bones of your letter or CV. As you can see in Mail-Shots 1 and 2, both authors have highlighted the benefits they could offer an employer.

A little creativity and a touch of imagination can bring even the most ordinary of career structures to red-blooded life.

7.

Preparing Your CV

A Curriculum Vitae, unlike a mailer, should say everything there is to say about you, your educational record and your employment background. But, as I said at the beginning of this book, it shouldn't simply be a long and turgid list of jobs done, schools attended and hobbies followed. On the contrary, it should be as creative as your mailer — and that applies not only to the content, but also to the design and layout — with the objectives behind your activities carefully argued.

Accomplishment is what employers look for. They need to see the benefit of employing you. This can be portrayed, for instance, with the dot and comma of sales achieved in previous jobs — the percentages and the revenue income — and how and why you achieved them.

Or, again, with the reasoning behind your attendance at evening classes, in order to bolster a solitary GCSE, and how the result of working for an HNC in secretarial studies will be worth its weight in gold to an employer.

Or, yet again, where a purely personal interest in the latest developments in micro-computer technology makes you an undisputed authority (albeit uncertificated) on data-base and spreadsheet software.

Practically anything you are interested in can be engineered to the advantage of an employer. Because — and remember this — past achievement is a copper-bottomed indicator of future performance. So spell it out... imaginatively.

I am acquainted with a young man who, until recently, had never been employed since leaving school three years earlier. He had no academic qualifications and no work experience. On the face of it, he had no prospects whatsoever.

Anyway, he told me he was applying for a job with a mail order firm as a junior despatch clerk; though he held out little hope. In conversation, I learned that he was a keen philatelist who had been collecting stamps since the age of 10. Further discussion revealed that he had an encyclopaedic knowledge of world geography (topographies, climates, populations, flora and fauna); the kind of knowledge that the average university lecturer would have killed for; all of it subconsciously learned in the pursuit of his hobby. I therefore told him to make a great play of this in his CV, which he was fairly reluctant to do, arguing that it was of little interest to anyone but himself. In the event, however, he did it.

At the subsequent interview, the firm's manager questioned my young friend about his hobby (to be honest, there was little else that could be talked about); and he was bowled over, not only with the lad's knowledge of foreign countries, but also with the painstaking methods he employed for collating and indexing his vast collection of stamps. So impressed was the manager, that he asked the lad to bring some samples of his collection along to a second interview.

He got the job — in the face of stiff opposition, too, from other youngsters with a healthy line in GCSEs and work experience certificates.

Why? Not only because his interest in geography could be turned to good use by the mail order firm, since its entire business revolved around despatching goods to places elsewhere. But also on the grounds that he put himself out to do something for which the reward was nothing more than self-satisfaction. Further, he got the job because he could demonstrate an aptitude and discipline for maintaining files and keeping records.

I later spoke to the percipient manager, who admitted that most of the other candidates were interested in little except themselves, pop music and the opposite sex. As far as he was concerned, there was no contest.

A fairly banal illustration, I'll admit. But a true one with a successful outcome. Demonstrating, I think, that no skill or ability should ever be considered beneath your dignity.

On the subject of CV design, you may find it worthwhile to approach one of the many secretarial agencies that specialise in CV production. They are usually equipped with IBM compatible or Apple-Mac computers, which are capable of a superb job.

Ownership of a computer, however, doesn't make the operator a designer or anything like it. So it may be prudent to rough out a design yourself and have the agency operator follow it. In any event, always ask to see what they have done for others — then judge. The same applies to content — write it yourself; and write it along the lines of what follows.

My example uses one of the earlier mailers as its basis. And while the additional information is purely imaginary, it gives you an idea of how seemingly mundane facts can be turned into interesting achievements. But, first, a rough draft of a covering letter to accompany the CV.

Dear Mr Cake,

With reference to your advertisement for a Sales Manager (The Daily News — 16th April), I should be obliged if you would consider the enclosed Curriculum Vitae in relation to the position outlined.

It may be prudent to mention that I have a provable record of success in Sales Management and have exceeded sales targets, both as a Manager and a Salesman, every year of my career.

I should also say that I would be unwilling to change my present position for anything less than a job of the dimension and challenge indicated in your advertisement.

I look foward to any interview you may care to grant.

Most sincerely,

Note the air of confidence exhibited by the 'writer'. No employer wants a cringer. Also, notice how the writer, via the words *dimension* and *challenge,* both congratulates Mr Cake for offering such a worthwhile job and suggests his own capacity for handling it.

Now for the CV.

CURRICULUM VITAE

Aaron A. G. String
17 Highwayman Close
Andover
Hampshire AN3 5ES

Telephone: 0909 223301

Presented to:

Mr C. D. Cake, Sales Director
Castle Plastics
Edinburgh EH45 8VW

CURRICULUM VITAE

**Aaron A. G. String
17 Highwayman Close
Andover
Hampshire AN3 5ES**

(Photograph)

Telephone: 0909 223301

CAREER
SUMMARY

In the past ten years, I have worked as a salesman and, latterly, as a Sales Manager in the chemicals industry. As Regional Sales Manager, heading a team of five salespeople, I increased sales of domestic rainwear and sub-surface products by 43% in just 18 months.

This was achieved by establishing a more substantial customer base; by developing existing accounts and introducing new clients; by launching customer promotions and discount packages; and by creating an innovative sales-training programme.

OBJECTIVE

Sales Director or Sales Training Manager for a national organisation manufacturing industrial plastics.

DATE
OF BIRTH

(Day, Month, Year.)

EDUCATION

BSc., Chemistry – Essex University (Year)

CAREER
HISTORY

(Year) –
Regional Sales Manager
Acme Polymers Ltd., Greenbank,
Andover, Hampshire AN10 9EW.

CAREER HISTORY (Contd.)	(Year) to (Year) Salesman Ajax Chemicals Ltd, Ajax House, Basingstoke, Hampshire BE34 2TK
	Duties included selling a range of oil-additives to the automotive industry.
	Developed the South East territory from a modest £350,000 nett sales area into £1.3 million in four years.
	This was achieved by increasing existing client sales by 30% and successfully prospecting a total of 170 new accounts.
	Calls and negotiations were made at executive and purchasing levels.
LANGUAGES	Working knowledge of French and German.
SPORT	Member of Andover Rugby Club.
COMMUNITY ACTIVITY	Chairman of the Andover Round Table. Recent activities include the provision of a Transit Van for the Andover Youth Society.
SOCIAL ACTIVITY	Member of the Andover Gliding Club.
PERSONAL	Married with two children.
HEALTH	Excellent.
REFEREES	John Goldblatt, Chief Flying Instructor, Andover Flying Club, Twelve Elms Airfield, Andover, AN7 4WS.
	Marion Stevens, Sales Director, Ajax Chemicals Ltd, Ajax House, Basingstoke, Hampshire BE34 2TK.

There is a school of thought which suggests that a CV should be no more than one page in length. This is one of those daft and unquantifiable rules just waiting to be broken. So, to hell with it, let's break it. I'm prepared to argue that a CV should be as long as it takes — with the proviso that what is being said is worth reading. So why restrict yourself to one page? Why, indeed? In the first place, a single page might be misconstrued as the work of someone who is either lazy or pinching pennies. In the second place, I feel that if you have something to say, then say it boldly or cleverly, or wittily or stridently, but never ever say it half-heartedly. You may take my word for it that there is an expression used in the advertising business when an agency is preparing a presentation for a client; and this expression runs: 'Let's throw some paper at them — and lots of it.'

I also take the view that any achievement, hobby or pastime is well worth mentioning. After all, you never know what might interest the person reading your piece. If he's into Morris Dancing and so are you, you can wager a fair slice of cash that he'll grant you an interview. Like they say, there's none so queer as folk.

Back to the CV.

I've employed reverse chronological order for the employment details in this example. It happens to be a nice way of getting your strengths over to the reader in the fastest possible way, along with instant information about your latest (and hopefully best) achievements. But if, say, you were hoping to change the direction of your career, then chronological order would be a better bet, since your most recent, and therefore inapplicable, job is left until last. This format gives the reader time to absorb your breadth of experience over the years and takes the emphasis off current employment.

Whichever you choose, try to stay away from the ego-tripping pronoun 'I' in the blurb. Or, at least, use as few as readability will allow. Further, quote percentages and other worthwhile statistics in numerals. A reader will remember a

'50% sales increase' more readily than a 'fifty per cent sales increase' − if you follow my drift.

IMPORTANT NOTE

Always include an OBJECTIVE (that is, your Career Objective) in a CV. It happens to be one of the most important elements, since it is a summary of your ambitions. Therefore, be relatively specific − with the emphasis on relatively. Do your best to refrain from going overboard with statements like: 'I intend to become Chairman of Barclays Bank within the year'. You'll be sending this same, printed or laser-printed CV to any number of prospects. So you don't want to rule yourself out of the running for any job which might be closely related to the one you are applying for, and which might soon come up for grabs.

Also, employ 'action' words when describing your achievements. Words like: 'created', 'increased', 'developed', 'launched', and so on.

Something else worth remembering is that you should organise your referees well in advance of CV preparation. It could be really embarrassing to have someone you nominated as a character referee, at best, denying your existence or, at worst, putting in the knife simply because you hadn't the courtesy to ask his permission.

You think I'm kidding? Not two days ago, I was told of someone who was put up as referee unasked. I won't go into detail about the reaction from said reluctant referee. Suffice, I think, to say that the bloke responsible failed even to get to first base with the job he wanted.

Once you've acquainted your referees with what you're about to do, try to give them some indication of the kind of companies that will contact them and, just for the record, give them a copy of your CV. It will give them some leads when the time comes to answer a prospective employer's questions.

However reluctant you may feel about asking, a past employer will almost always give you a decent reference — no matter how angry was your parting. I mean, were he to give you a duff citation, his face could end up redder than yours. After all, if you were *that* terrible, how come he hired you in the first place?

What about the problems of asking your *present* employer for a reference? By that I mean asking for a reference immediately after telling him that you are in the process of looking for a new job. I mention it only because a potential employer might want to know what you are thought of by the firm currently paying your wages. It happens. Infrequently, I'll grant; but it happens.

Well, it could be that you have already reached an agreement with your current boss that you have gone as far as you can with him, and a change would be in your interests. If this is the case, if your relationship with him is a good one, you are unlikely to be thrown out before you are ready to go. Conversely, where there is no real love lost, it might be wiser to keep your plans to yourself.

I can give you a personal example of what I'm talking about. Early on in my career, while working for a London ad agency, I was approached by another agency with a tempting job offer that not only promised a large increase in salary, but also wider opportunities. I accepted the offer; but such is the nature of the advertising game — where some unscrupulous types claim authorship of work they haven't done — I had to prove that the specimen work I showed at the interview was, indeed, my own. To achieve this, I was forced to approach my boss for a proof to that effect. He could either write or phone the potential employer.

Our subsequent chat was not one I looked forward to. But, after explaining what I was doing and what I needed, my employer looked me straight in the eye and said, 'For my part... stay. For your own benefit... go. I'll speak to this crew now.'

As in all things, honesty is the best policy; but never stick your chin out unnecessarily.

In the past few months, I have read more CVs than you could wave a wand at; and many of these go out of their way to give reasons for leaving previous jobs. 'Advancement' is a word that crops up time and time again; but it's an empty word and conveys little. It speaks volumes, however, about the fact that the writer was somehow unable to 'advance' with the said firm; and that tends to beg the question: how come?

Of course, we all know that most people change jobs out of sheer frustration, or total boredom, or because of personality clashes with colleagues. But it's unwise to lay this out in black and white. On balance, I'd say omit any reference to 'reasons for leaving'. You can always produce an acceptable reason if asked at an interview. Omission can no way be classed as fibbing.

If you don't have a past employer, ask a teacher or a youth club leader to act as a character referee. Under no circumstances, and I mean strictly no circumstances, nominate your probation officer. That could open a whole new line in pub chat for the recipient of your CV. *Now* I'm kidding!

IMPORTANT NOTE

If you have a congratulatory First from Oxford, you shouldn't bother to list your school exam grades. But if you don't, then take care to present them all: including music diplomas and swimming certificates — the lot.

You may be asking why I've suggested the inclusion of a photograph in the sample CV. All right. I'll tell you why. It's for the same reason that newspapers include a photograph of a newsworthy, but hitherto unknown, person in many items. It's for the same reason that advertisers include an illustration of their product in a press ad. And the reason is this:

A photograph in a news item puts the reader face to face with the subject of that item. When someone is described as 'the genial, 45-year-old host of the Horse & Groom Inn, who has barred the Chancellor of the Exchequer from his premises on the grounds of rowdyism', we are delighted to see a picture of this eminently sensible and ostensibly likeable man.

Again, an illustration of a product in an ad shows you exactly what you are being asked to shell out hard-earned cash to own. It's a well-researched fact that an all-type ad usually has much less impact than a similar ad complete with pic of the goods in question.

We've said it before. You have a whole wide range of products to sell: experience, ideas, diligence, know-how — you name it. And although you don't have to subscribe to the romantic novelists' concept that a person's character and experiences are written in their face, it's certainly true that a photograph, when taken in conjunction with what is written in a CV, is likely, in its effect, to be more positive than negative. The personnel manager, or whoever is the arbiter, will have more affinity with you, since he somehow feels that he already knows you. What's more, he sees that you have taken that extra bit of trouble by including a pic... and that can only work in your favour.

As the man said: 'It's awfully hard to shift product without offering it for sale'. So offer it for sale — graphically.

And that's a long-winded way of saying: include a photograph. A decent one, that is; not one of these instant passport jobs. Most people using passport booths end up looking like they should be helping the police with their enquiries.

Use spray mount or double-sided sticky tape to fix it neatly to the CV.

I guess you don't need me to tell you that when you are making an unsolicited submission to a company, you should direct your CV and covering letter to a nominee in the Personnel Department (where one exists), or to the Department Head of the division in which you are interested.

A phone-chat with the firm's receptionist will unearth the names you need. Don't do what many do: which is to send the thing off to the company in general rather than a person in particular. These get passed disinterestedly from department to department and finish up in a convenient waste-bin — if they get passed at all.

At this point, I want to shoot off at a tangent to tell you an effervescent little story. The main players are a large and popular wine-bar, located in one of our larger cities, and a young lady who was sick and tired of having her job applications rejected. Well, the wine-bar advertised for a full-time waiter/waitress and, as you'd expect, received several hundred replies. The great proportion of these were, remarkably enough, from recent graduates; but they were pretty scruffy affairs, written on scraps of paper torn from note books and such. There was one, however, which stood out like a large Scotch on a Temperance Hall tea-trolley. It came in the shape of a greetings card, of the sort that can be bought in most decent newsagents. The front cover was a nicely-painted scene depicting a French bistro, while the inside pages held the lady's hand-written career details.

She was hired immediately.

I cannot emphasise enough the importance of rising out of the ordinary and making your applications extraordinary — like this one was. In the advertising game they call such a device a 'stopper'; and it comes in the shape of a startling headline or a startling illustration, or both. Its effect is to stand out from the mass and belt you right between the eyes. Stoppers take the reader by delicious surprise, forcing him to pursue the rest of the material at length.

I hope I'm not labouring this point, but it is important.

In the last two chapters we've covered three distinct methods of solicitation:

1. The mail-shot or unsolicited trawl letter.

2. The CV and covering letter in response to an ad.

3. The unsolicited CV and covering letter.

Methods 1 and 3 will take up a lot of your time and a great deal of paper. Nonetheless, when they are done with imagination and confidence, they can and do engender positive responses. (There are additional examples of mail-shots and covering letters elsewhere in this book. More importantly, perhaps, I have outlined some tried-and-tested methods showing *how* to write them.)

All things being equal, one or other of the methods should fetch an interview appointment.

Let's keep that appointment.

8.

Interview Techniques

The first thing to know about the questions that an interviewer will ask you is that there are no *right* answers — only answers that help him to evaluate whether you are worthy of an offer of employment.

In this respect, he is attempting to discover the following:

1. Your accomplishments.

2. Your strengths.

3. Your ability to gel within the company.

4. Your potential for promotion.

Of these, the most important are 1 and 2. Your
accomplishments are a good bench-mark for how you will
perform in the future. While your strengths determine how
well you will acquit yourself if he offers you the job.

It really is that simple.

So, in answering these questions, you should be as honest
and as lucid as the circumstances permit. Only a masochist
would not be nervous in an interview situation. (There can't be
too many people capable of walking into a room, knowing that
what they say in the next sixty minutes will determine their
lives into the foreseeable future, without experiencing a few
butterflies.)

Now, while I have said that there are no right answers, there
are certainly a lot of *wrong* ones; and an experienced
interviewer can spot these three miles away. Indeed, the major
part of his job is to look for the danger signals which
instinctively tell him that the subject of his enquiry is not all
he purports to be.

Here's what they look for, and what makes them think twice,
and then think again, about making an offer.

1. An interviewee who complains about his present or past
   employer/colleagues/working conditions.

      The interviewer knows that, before long, this person
   will be complaining likewise about him.

2. The candidate who talks about salary before he knows the
   full dimensions of the job.

      This character is more interested in what he can get out
   of a job than what he might put in.

3. An interviewee who lists a plethora of short-stay jobs in
   his CV.

      He may, of course, have been under-challenged and
   therefore intellectually frustrated. On the other hand, he
   may just be unemployable.

4. People who try to paper over certain obvious cracks in
   their career and sidestep questions in this area.

Practically everyone has had periods in their lives when idleness, stupidity, wanderlust, 'bad luck', or even prison, has prevented them from following their regular course. Almost nobody will admit it in public, and very few even in private. Though only an immature fool will not admit it to himself. And likewise for anyone who attends an interview and doesn't prepare a watertight cover-story!

5. A candidate with little or no interest in outside activities in the shape of hobbies, pastimes, sports and socializing.

This guy purports to live only for his work. Is he, by any chance, an apprentice hermit or just brain-dead?

The experienced interviewer also keeps his eyes open for visual danger signs. We'll talk about those in a later chapter.

In very small organisations, interviewing is pretty much a hit-and-miss affair, with the outcome dependent on the manager's personal quirks and foibles, rather than upon the interviewee's suitability for the job. The managers at such firms often have no training in interview techniques and therefore work by instinct.

In larger organisations, though, you'll come up against professional personnel management types. These men and women don't allow their own feelings of like and dislike for certain types of people to interfere with professional judgment.

The former have little or no system, while the latter work to a set format, awarding candidates plus or minus points within that framework. The points are then assessed, and the half-dozen top scorers go onto a shortlist for second interview.

In order to assist collating the points, an interviewer will use a form of assessment similar to the one reproduced here.

Knowing that, as you sit across the desk from your interviewer, he is assessing your answers and completing a table of this kind, should make you feel quite happy. For one thing, people become nervous when an interviewer makes notes in their presence, but out of their view; now there is no longer any mystery to it. For another, knowing what scores positive points will help you to set up positive answers.

I think we should spend some time, now, looking at typical questions that interviewers ask, along with guides to positive responses. You may also consider it a good idea, once you have taken the responses on board, to ask a friend/wife/husband/parent to read this section and then check out your ad lib answers to the same questions. If they can handle it, they might be prepared to complete the Candidate Assessment form — with plus and minus points out of 10 beside each category. Obviously, most categories require several questions to be posed before a hard and fast conclusion can be arrived at.

The following questions and their guideline responses are loosely framed — and deliberately so. Your particular achievements and circumstances will be totally different from the next person's.

Qualifications & Experience Questions

Q. *What are your professional strengths?*

A. Motivating others.
   Working with the minimum of supervision.

Q. *Why do you want to leave your present job?*

A. I need:
   Greater challenges.
   More responsibility.
   Better opportunities.
   Wider experience of my field.
   My present job does not stretch me enough. I feel that I'm ready for wider responsibilities.
   (Never, ever, because you have fallen out with your boss or a colleague. The response must be positive, not negative.)

Q. *Bearing in mind your qualifications, why isn't your salary a lot higher?*

CANDIDATE ASSESSMENT

Qualifications & Experience	Knowledge & Skills	Personality	Personal Attitude	Personal Circumstances	Score Neg.	Pos.
Academic achievements	Abilities required	To tackle job	Power hungry	Right age		
Potential	Skill to create those abilities	To join team	Money motivated	Home stability		
Experience desirable	Decision making	Leader	Attitude to authority	Appearance		
Experience essential	Ability to use judgment	Follower	Need for challenge	Speech quality		
Related experience	Logical	Articulate	Attitude to subordinates	Driving licence		
				TOTALS		

A. I've been striving for experience. Money has been a secondary consideration. Now I'm looking for a salary to match my ability.

Q. *How much do you know about this company?*
(This is where homework pays off.)

A. I know the history of the company.
I am familiar with the company's products and markets, and have researched those of your competitors.
I also have details of declared profits and have a fair idea of the company's growth potential.
Which area do you wish me to speak about?
(All this information can be found in the company's Annual Report and product literature.)

Q. *If you could begin again, what changes would you make?*
(The interviewer is trying to find out whether you honestly enjoy what you do.)

A. I would have *improved* myself:
by specializing in... (a certain area)
by diversifying into... (given areas)
or by taking relevant courses in... (name subjects)
(depending on your circumstances).

Q. *What new systems or programmes have you implemented in your present job?*
(He wants to know how creative or innovative you are.)

In explaining anything you've done, bear in mind the candidate profile this company has outlined, and try to make your answer conform to it.

Q. *Can you work under pressure?*

(This is a throwaway question which has only a 'yes, I can' answer. But back it up, where possible, with examples of how you have worked to tight deadlines.)

Q. *You have a very important decision to make. How do you go about it?*
(He's probing your analytical processes.)

A. If it must be my decision alone, I think the problem through, write down the pros and cons, and arrive at a solution which best suits the company's interests. Though if this decision will affect the working practices of others, I should seek their opinions, and then make up my mind. (Now you're displaying leadership qualities.)

Q. *How would you feel about having a younger man or woman as your boss?*

A. It makes no difference if they are younger. Nor, indeed, am I concerned whether they are male or female. My only concern is with their ability and whether I can learn from them.

Q. *You've had so many jobs in such a short time. How can we be sure that you will stay with us?*

A. I have been exploring my career objectives; and I believe that my goals could be achieved with this company.

Alternatively:
Each job change has been made to achieve more responsibility and to widen my career horizons. I am, however, aware that this company awards effort with promotion. Therefore, it will be in both our interests if I stay.

Q. *You've been in your present position for a long time. Won't it be difficult to adjust to a new company?*

A. Absolutely not. Over the years, I have worked with a wide variety of people, all with different attitudes and motivations. Thus, the change will come as no surprise.

Q. *What will you be doing in 2 years from now?*

(This question almost always arises and you should have a well-rehearsed summary of your career objectives ready to deliver. These should obviously be framed in relation to the job being applied for.)

A. If I earn the responsibilities I am hoping for from this organisation, then in 2 years I shall be...

IMPORTANT NOTE

The older you are, the less importance will be placed on academic qualifications. And if you are going for a senior position, schooling is unlikely even to be mentioned.

If asked awkward questions about your lack of academic achievement, however, try to emphasize your leadership qualities and any activities which demonstrate your commitment to career goals.

Q. *You don't have a degree. You have no school-leaving certificates. Why?*

A. I think my work experience makes up fully for my lack of educational qualifications.
(To this may be added — if true):

My circumstances were such that I had to bring money into the household. Given the choice, I would certainly have taken further education.

I am literate and numerate enough to have acquitted myself well in previous jobs.

Q. *You are under-qualified for this job. What makes you think you can tackle it?*

A. I am quick on the uptake. I learn fast. To prove it, allow me to give you an example of what I achieved in my present/last job...

Q. *You are over-qualified for this job. Your experience is beyond what the post calls for.*

A. True — but just think about the contribution I will be able to make. And there will be no time wasted batting myself in.

What's more, I shall be able to bring a brand new perspective to the job.

Personality & Personal Questions

Q. *What was the title of the last book you read?*
What do you do in your spare time?

(These questions are used to develop a rapport between interviewer and interviewee. Keep your eyes open and note any books, photographs or sports equipment on or near the interviewer's desk. There may just be a mutual point of interest close at hand.

However, if he has a drinks cabinet in the office, it would be unwise to suggest that, by the looks of things, you have a hobby in common; so let's push the boat out!)

Q. *What is your idea of success?*

A. A successful person, in my opinion, is one who makes a real contribution to the company's profitability. Someone, also, who provides well for his family and does some good in the community.

Q. *I don't like people who boast. What irritates you about other people?*

A. Well, I recognise that we all have failings; so I take people as they come. I do my best to get along with everyone and don't get involved in office politics.

Q. *What do you think people find irritating in you?*

A. Plenty, I imagine. But possibly my biggest fault is my tendency to be over-enthusiastic about projects.

    (Brilliantly done! Always make your faults agreeable to an employer.)

Q. *Let me pose a hypothetical situation. The Managing Director makes a statement about your department, in front of others, that you know to be wrong. How would you confront this situation?*

A. If I felt that the statement was to have no direct or derogatory effect upon the company, I should not confront it at all. If, on the other hand, I saw that his statement might harm the company, I would wait until I could confront him alone and then, as diplomatically as possible, point out the error.

IMPORTANT NOTE

If you don't understand a question, then say so. Never attempt to answer a question that you don't quite follow − you'll only end up looking foolish. If a question is unclear, simply say something like: 'I'm sorry, I'm a little slow today. I don't think I understand the question'.

And if the interviewer says something like: 'Are you acquainted with Victor Hugo?', don't say yes if you aren't; because the next question will almost certainly ask just *how* acquainted you are − and that could result in an embarrassment which could lose you the job. Never agree that you know something if you don't.

Q. *How would you describe your personality?*

A. This question also comes in the form of 'Tell me about yourself' or 'Do you have any close friends?' (Friends tend to resemble each other; thus, in talking about a friend, you may also be describing yourself.)

To answer this question, you need to have a crack at the Character Appraisal on page 30.

Q. *Have you lately decided on any new personal objectives?*

Here's the opportunity to show that there's more to you than meets the eye. Spell out your plans — the career goals as well as the personal ones. Things like:

(a) You've enrolled at night school for a language course. This will be of benefit to any company trading in the EC.

(b) You're building your own home, garage, conservatory, or restoring a classic car. This kind of project demonstrates self-motivation.

(c) You're training to run a marathon for charity.

Mention anything and everything that shows you have a little bit of get-up-and-go.

Q. *What if I tell you that, should you be given this job, your immediate boss is a perfectionist who doesn't suffer fools gladly? How do you react?*

A. Until I meet him, that's impossible to say. But he is clearly good at what he does, otherwise you wouldn't employ him. On those grounds, I'd hope to gain his trust and work closely with him.

Q. *If you are given this job, you will be taking over a department staffed by very young people. Some of them are half your age. How do you feel about that?*

A. With the right motivation, young people are happy to learn new tricks. Unlike old dogs. My experience and know-how should help provide that motivation.

Q. *How do you feel about delegating responsibility?*

A. Comfortable. While I would be responsible for the
   outcome of the tasks in question, I am happy to let others
   make their own decisions on how they get them done. I
   think people are ten times more effective when they are
   given free rein.

IMPORTANT NOTE

If you are applying for an 'office-bound' job in one of
the traditional professions — solicitor's office, shipping
company, bank — your motivation should appear to be
for the contribution you can make towards the quality of
service offered by the company, and for the long-term
security.

Where you're after a job in one of the 'creative'
businesses — architecture, advertising, journalism — the
incentive must seem to be more towards your ability to
donate valuable skills to the art and craft of the trade,
with just a soupçon of concern for maintaining the
company's profitability.

But where you are chasing a job in sales, be
mercenary. Make money your motivation and riches your
goal. Nine times out of ten, a sales manager has real
empathy with the cash-oriented applicant.

Q. *How do you feel about being delegated to?*

A. Again, comfortable. Given a firm objective, I would
   complete the task without further reference to the
   delegator.

Q. *Finally, is there anything you wish to ask me?*

A. Yes — would you like me to start in two weeks or four?
   But seriously, it is imperative that you prepare a few

questions to ask at this point. And now I come to think about it, you should have a few up your sleeve to put to the interviewer as the meeting progresses.

An interview should not be a non-return valve, with all the questions going one way. When you interject questions of your own, you are demonstrating intelligence and perspicacity — not to mention the importance you place on your career.

Apart from anything else, you can take your turn at putting someone through the wringer.

What kind of questions should you ask? Queries about the company, its products or plans for growth ('I understand you are diversifying into the consumer market. What effect will this have on sales of your industrial products?') are better than self-related questions like: 'If I am appointed, what kind of pension package can I expect?'

Such questions as: 'Why is this position open?' and 'The person who had this position — what is he doing now?' are good for breaking the initial ice. As is 'Why have you chosen to recruit from outside for this position, rather than internally?' It is never prudent to ask what hapened to the last person to hold the job, but this information may be volunteered in answer to either of these questions.

More importantly, you can highlight your own strengths with seemingly innocuous questions. You make an innocent inquiry about the company's progress within an area that you excel. Something like: 'I imagine that all your sales and stock records are computerised?' When the manager replies, either in the affirmative or negative, you say: 'That's interesting, because in my present job I was responsible for installing specially-written software that...'

The higher up the employment scale you are, the more important are your questions. Have 'em ready.

For obvious reasons, managers will hire people they can get along with. Well-framed questions from you help remove the formality from the meeting and put you on the road to establishing a rapport with your interrogator.

As was intimated earlier, you never ask questions about the

type of business the company is in, or the range of products it sells. You should already know practically everything there is to know about the company. If it's in the public domain, it should be in your head.

Anyone who turns up at an interview without a concise knowledge of the company is either a very confident interviewee — or a very stupid one.

Some Points to Ponder

In an interview, how you respond is as important as what you respond. You need to be articulate without appearing excitable. Mumbling, prefixing every statement with an 'um' or an 'er' and nervous articulation will create a bad impression, no matter how well qualified you may be.

So learn your lines. Rehearse your responses aloud. Never mind your regional accent; it's clarity and credibility you're after.

Like this, there is no question they can ask for which you can't tailor an answer. Like this, too, you'll never be scratching around for a plausible answer.

Also, be flexible. Interviewers tend to jump around from subject to subject. Be ready for the surprise question near the close of the meeting, when the interviewer tries to rattle your confidence.

Large organisations sometimes retain a psychologist in their personnel department. This fellow will be rather more interested in your personal attitudes, your demeanour and long-term plans than your technical qualifications. In a committee-type interview, where you face several people at once, you can identify him readily enough by the slant of his questions. And once you've nailed him, look him straight in the eye, refrain from waving your hands around, bowing your head, talking into your chest or shuffling your feet. If you act mature and self-secure, he can do little else but give you a good report. Like this, you have gained at least one ally.

A certain type of interviewer delights in putting you under stress. He will constantly interrupt your answers; he will contradict you and try to demonstrate a superior understanding of your particular field. Now and again, he will appear genuinely bellicose.

This often occurs when there is more than one interviewer present.

Don't let this type faze you. Keep your head. Refrain from arguing. Make your points as lucidly as the interruptions will allow. Don't be drawn into making rash statements. The attitude to take is embodied in the philosophy of the judo masters: the bamboo bends with the wind, but never breaks.

Many years ago, I attended an interview for a freelance writing assignment where the sadist in charge sat me opposite a large window through which the brilliant morning sunshine shone right into my eyes. I made the mistake of asking him if I could move. He refused the request point-blank and I had to endure being half-blinded for the duration of the interview.

I now know that I should have moved to another chair without breaking the conversation, and without asking. Apparently, he was testing my self-confidence.

The job went to someone else — probably to someone a lot more mature.

On another occasion, I went after a very big copywriting job in a large London advertising agency. The interview was conducted by the copy chief and two designers. Within about five minutes, I was asked if I played liar-dice, which I did. The next two hours were taken up by a series of games in which I studiously lost most of the cash in my wallet. Finally, the trio decided it was home-time and we departed, with a promise from the copy chief that he would get in touch.

He wrote to me — and the gist of his letter was that he had hired a better copywriter.

Three months later, the job was advertised yet again. The new writer had not come up to scratch. I wrote to the copy chief: 'I have a tenner to lose. Any chance of a game?' I was hired. And the copy chief turned out to be not only the most talented ad man I've ever met, but also an unconscionably decent bloke.

Which proves that some people have truly bizarre ideas about how to conduct interviews, and you should be ready for them.

Some interviewers never seem to get around to the interview. They talk sport, politics, sex — you name it. You, of course, join in.

Careful. This fellow will learn more about you from your improvised responses to a statement about the clay-footedness of politicians than he will do from hearing your rehearsed lines on how well you can do the job in question. He wants to know whether you can work with him, or fit into the company's scheme of things. Further, he may be luring you into a sense of false security. Any minute now he will deliver the punch question that might take you off guard and put you out of the running.

Another ploy that interviewers adopt is to introduce long silences between questions. For example, when you have answered up neatly and concisely to a given question, then your man just sits there staring at you. You feel uncomfortable. You are scrabbling around in your mind for something to add.

Should you try to fill the gap? Absolutely not.

In such circumstances you might blurt something out for which there is no justification or necessity, and for which you may later kick yourself. Stay *stumm*. He's testing your self-restraint. Stare back at him. It is, after all, *his* turn.

There are some queer fish about. There's the one who bluntly says: 'Frankly, I don't think you're up to this job.' And another who goes on at tedious lengths about how perfect you are for the position and what an asset you'd be to the company. Both are seeking a response from you.

Make sure it's the one they want.

Of course, you won't know how to play it until you get there and have met the interviewer. As I've said, all interviewers are individual, yet some are more individual than others. But something I'd like you to keep in mind is this. There is a saying in the advertising business which goes: 'When flannel fails, try flattery.'

I have lost count of the times that, during a presentation of proposed ideas to a client, when it is clear he is not agreeing with anything I have to say or show, I have heard myself saying: 'We knew you would have reservations about this, Mr X. But let's be truthful, we aren't selling this product to people with an IQ as high as yours patently is...'

Additional Questions for Women

For reasons that are self-evident, interviewers have an entire portfolio of questions specifically reserved for women candidates. Whether it is right or wrong, politically correct or otherwise, sexist or not, I don't know and wouldn't care to speculate. It's a fact, all the same. So here are a few, a very few, of those that crop up, along with some ways of countering them.

Q. Do you have any plans for getting married?

A. (If you do.) Certainly. As a matter of fact we've set the date for August next year. However, being married will have no effect upon my career whatsoever.

Q. Does your husband approve of you working?

A. Yes, most certainly. We both wish to fulfill ourselves with our careers.

Q. Do you plan to have (more) children?

A. At the moment − no.

(Don't dither, don't sound undecided, don't leave room for the interviewer to have doubts.)

Q. The position involves the supervision of male staff. How do you feel about that?

A. Exactly as I would about supervising female staff. I am only interested in performance.

Q. If your husband's company wanted him to relocate to
    another office, outside the county — what would you do?

A. I should go with him, of course.

(Any other answer to this question is sure to be looked upon
with suspicion — mainly, because it would be thought unlikely
or, alternatively, because it will bring the stability of your
home life into question.)

And now for something completely different. But
desperately important. It applies to everyone.
You will neglect to read this bit to your permanent regret.

NOW READ THIS

There is a popular game in the advertising industry that goes under the name of: 'Let's write to them before they write to us.' It is played like this. When any given agency visits a client, or when any given client visits an agency, both the visitors and the hosts rush back to their respective offices and dash off a rapid letter of thanks. The party of the first part says: 'Thanks for having us', while the party of the second part says: 'How nice of you to drop in.' The fact that these letters are despatched for nothing more than mercenary reasons is not up for discussion. But the fact that a nice warm glow is felt by both the writers and the recipients most certainly is.

Which is why I urge you, once you have attended your interview, *to write to the interviewer concerned and thank him or her for giving you their valuable time.*

A gambit of this kind could work wonders – and in more ways than one:

1. It will make the interviewer feel more important than he already feels he is.

2. It will set you aside in the interviewer's mind from the great mass of other applicants. Very, very few of whom will have taken the bother to write.

3. It will demonstrate that you are thoughtful and, therefore, likely to fit in – both with your potential colleagues and the firm's clients.

4. It will show that you know a thing or two about salesmanship. (The clever salesman doesn't make a call on a prospect and then disappear for six months – he follows up in person and with mailers... often.)

5. Where the interviewer is maybe dithering between choosing yourself and one other applicant, it may just push him into acting in your favour.

6. And in the event that you don't get the job, a letter of thanks will stand you in good stead for

any other position that might arise in the future. (I'll wager a fair shade of odds that you will be remembered.)

Something along the following lines might be in order:

Dear Mr Boat,

I must thank you, indeed, for taking the time to see me yesterday. I much enjoyed our meeting and feel confident that something positive will come of it.

I truly believe that I possess both the qualifications and the demeanour for the post. What is more, I am keen to show how well I can acquit myself.

However, should you care to know more or see more, please do not hesitate to get in touch. I can be contacted, at any time, at the above number.

Most sincerely,

April Schauers

Pushy? Certainly.
Self-assured? No question.
Cocky? You'd better believe it!

9.

How To See What Others Are Thinking

There are some among us who say that the 'science' of body language is somewhat akin to those other obscure 'sciences' water divining and extra sensory perception. The hang-up seems to be that each of us has to have the phenomenon proved, before our very eyes, before we will believe it.

As someone who has seen a water diviner in action, I can tell you that my initial scepticism melted like snow off a dyke. I actually watched a neighbouring farmer trace the run of an underground water-pipe across several fields. The pipe was at least three feet below the surface, was made of cast-iron, and had been in the ground since the early 1900s. Unfortunately, there was no map of its directional progress in existence. Hence the divining act.

Subsequent sample digs proved the diviner right in every particular.

I have never had ESP demonstrated to my satisfaction; though my wife does a particularly good line in mind-reading when I've been in the pub with cronies and try to deny the fact. However, I think this has more to do with familiarity than unexplained phenomena.

Notwithstanding all of this, there is no doubt in my mind that the transmission and interpretation of body language is as real for those who have eyes to see it as the transmission and reception of radio waves. And the more I learn about it, the more convinced I am of its efficacy. For those who shrug it off as a matter of little consequence, I would point out (just as a 'for instance') that the early demonstrations of electricity, by Faraday and others, brought similar scoffers out of the woodwork. They saw it as no more than a party trick. Well — you live and learn, eh?

While putting this part of the book together, I was introduced to a lady who does research work at one of our more productive provincial universities. She had a lot to say on the subject of body language, and I will now sketch out her ideas.

To start with, there is nothing new about the study of non-verbal behaviour in human beings. One of the earliest researchers of the modern world was none other than Charles Darwin. His book: *The Expression of the Emotions in Man and Animals* came out in 1872. Since then, workers in the field have identified the staggering total of almost one million non-verbal expressions and cues.

Next, my informant suggested that something like 70% of communication exchanges are via the language of the body, rather than the spoken word. The fact that you don't know you are giving and receiving these cues is neither here nor there. Just because you aren't trained to recognise them, or don't know how to conceal them, it doesn't follow that they aren't happening. Thus, to a perceptive observer, you may be saying a good deal more than you wish to say.

'You can prove the principle of it,' she observed, 'with a simple experiment. Look into a mirror, then say "no" out loud, while simultaneously nodding your head. Then try saying "yes" while shaking your head from side to side. It can be done, yet it feels distinctly odd; and it seems to demonstrate that the body can exert some kind of subtle will over the brain. Biologists, of course, know it to be the other way around — with the brain in charge of the body. Yet it's by no means the whole story. What seems to happen is this. In body language, the body interprets and sends out signals transmitted to it by the unconscious, as opposed to the conscious, mind.

'So your mouth says: "I am very interested in what you are telling me"; while your body says: "If I don't get away from this character soon, I'll go nuts!"'

Not unremarkably, it is thought that women have a better awareness and a stronger perception of body language. Who knows, it may very well be the basis of that famous female intuition? Actors use it, of course, and in varying degrees of competence. In bad, or wooden, acting, it is easy to spot dialogue that doesn't match the body talk. The ability to make both correspond, and therefore be believable, results in the difference between the likes of an Anthony Hopkins and some of the characters in a well-known television soap opera — who, but for the laws of libel, I would cheerfully name.

Possibly the best manipulators of body language are politicians. It must take years of practice to tell a blatant, 100% proof, double-dyed lie to a potential 60 million people without giving the game away with contradictory body signals. That they can, and do, carry off a terrible fib with absolute plausibility cannot be in question; and in those terms our collective hats should go off to them.

As it happens, a full study of body language would require an entire book. For our purposes, though, we shall look to the basics of it and employ only those facts which may help us conceal the bad cues and broadcast the good in any interview situation.

We shall concern ourselves only with facial cues, hand and arm cues, and feet cues, since these are the most interpretable.

It appears that while many body cues are learned gestures, others are genetic. The way you fold your arms for instance — is it right over left, or left over right? Before you try it, think about it; and I shall be surprised if you can accurately describe your own version. How about the process of donning a coat? If you put it on right arm first, you're probably male; if it's left arm into the sleeve, then you are almost certainly female.

Again, many body gestures speak for themselves. In this vein, I offer the shoulder shrug, the smile, the grimace and the frown. Also, the thumbs up, the beckon and the wave. Others, however, are somewhat more subtle, but nonetheless interpretable.

When a woman shows interest in a man, she transmits what is described as a courtship cluster of signals. The smooth skin of the wrists, which has long been considered an erotic area, is exposed to the male. At the same time, the palms of the hands may be exposed, the head may be tossed, she may gaze at him through lowered lids, and her legs (whether she is sitting or standing) may be slightly, but noticeably, parted. It may also be noted that the head toss and the exposed wrist gesture are often employed by homosexual males.

In the case of a man interested in a woman, the stomach is pulled in — to emphasise muscle tone — and the shoulders are raised to emphasise height. This may be followed by preening gestures of tie being straightened, hair being smoothed and jacket being buttoned.

Anyhow, the first thing you are likely to do at an interview is shake hands with the interrogator. You may not know it, but your handshake counts for a lot — and I'm not only talking about the firmness, or otherwise, of it either. Further, your hands will say a lot about you as the meeting progresses.

We'll start with the handshake.

In the top pic of Figure 1, the shakers are on even terms, but in the bottom pic, the man on the left is exerting his

Fig 1.   The normal shake (top). The Dominant Shake (bottom).

dominance: after initial contact, his hand has turned so as to put him on top. This is a classic dominance gesture which, incidentally, can be taken to extreme lengths by actually offering the hand knuckles upward.

The handshake does not have the same impact when delivered between two women, or between a woman and a man. Even so, a wet and sweaty handshake, or one that's so limp as to need splints, can be detected by everyone and interpreted by everyone. Wet and sweaty means nervous or out of condition. Limp means wimp.

The moral, then, is to greet your interviewer with a firm shake, a dry shake and, depending on whether you can carry the same attitude right through the interview, a dominant one.

While we are at the handshake stage, maybe a word about

'territorial boundaries' would be in order. Just as countries have borders to delineate their national areas, so do human beings. Ours are not marked by customs' posts and police barriers, since they are quite imaginary; though they are, paradoxically, very real.

It seems that each of us has, all around us, an invisible 'air-space' which goes with us wherever we go. It's our personal territory; and when someone invades it uninvited, we become uncomfortable, irritable or downright aggressive — according to the type of character we are.

The radius of this air-space depends on which kind of society we live in; and it differs greatly from country to country. Generally speaking, if we were brought up in a city, then the space is smaller than if we were raised in a rural area. City dwellers are used to crowded conditions.

In addition, the air-space is, itself, divided into a number of zones.

Fig 2.   Zones and their distances.

The Public Zone represents the minimum distance we choose to stand from others if we are addressing them en masse i.e. at a public meeting.

The Social Zone is the distance we keep from people like shopkeepers, sales people, tradesmen and strangers generally.

The Personal Zone is our limit when attending a social gathering, like a reception or cocktail party.

The Intimate Zone. We allow nobody to intrude into this intimate space except parents, lovers and children.

From this we can see that getting too close to an interviewer might cause him to go on the defensive. While staying too far away might give the impression that we are stand-offish. The golden rule is keep your distance, but don't be too distant. A tried-and-tested gambit in interviews is to try gradually to close the gap between you and the interrogator as time progresses. Like this, he or she will feel an empathy developing towards you.

Next, let's look at palms.

When you are being truthful, you tend to offer your palms for inspection. People who are about to lie, invariably hide their palms — either in pockets, or behind their backs, or in

Fig 3.   'Let me be totally honest about this' palm gesture.

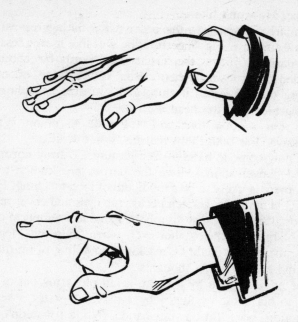

Fig 4. The Dominant Palm (above). The Aggressive Palm (below).

an arm-fold. This doesn't mean to say that everyone who shows you their palms is being completely honest. Some can do it while simultaneously verbalizing the biggest porkie since Richard Nixon denied knowing anything about the Watergate burglaries.

On the face of it, though, the palms up signal is a powerful show of frankness. Use it, and use it often.

Contrariwise, the palms down gesture is a dominance cue; as is the hand closed into a semi-fist, with the index finger pointing at the listener.

The next time you ask someone to do something for you, give the order with a palm down indicator (Fig 4). If he considers himself to be your equal, or even your superior, you will probably notice a very old-fashioned look flitting across his face. He won't like it.

Similarly, if you give the order using the aggressive palm (pointed finger — Fig 4) gesture, he will like it even less. And particularly so if you emphasise your words by jabbing the extended finger towards them. What you're doing, effectively, is using that finger as a club; and you are, metaphorically, banging him over the head with it.

As your mother told you, it's rude to point. It's also aggressive. For both these reasons, don't do it.

We now come to hand-to-face gestures. During normal and relaxed conversation, where the parties are known to each other, there is likely to be a modicum of face-touching. Fingers will tug at earlobes, scratch necks, rub eyes and cover mouths. Any, or all of these, may simply be genuine attempts to control an itch. In an interview, however, where there is a degree of stress, these cues could be masking the telling of untruths, or covering embarrassing thoughts.

The advice given by a padre to an old army pal of mine, prior to his being evaluated by a psychiatrist for a sensitive promotion, was: 'Sit on your hands.' While I wouldn't advise anyone actually to go ahead and sit on their hands, since it tends to make the sitter look a little idiotic, I would certainly go along with the essence of the padre's counsel. Keep your hands away from your face.

With any luck, though, nobody will have told the interviewer to do likewise. I therefore see no good reason why you shouldn't use what you know to evaluate his responses to you.

The fellow in Fig 5 is weighing up what you have to say. He may first stroke his chin, which indicates evaluation. But when the index finger lies on the jawbone, with the middle finger touching the upper lip, those thoughts could well be negative. And if, during this gesture, he leans right back in his seat, legs extended and ankles locked, you can almost bank on it that he isn't buying your act: which should tip you off either to reinforce what you've said, or change tack altogether.

Fig 5.   Critical (often negative) evaluation.

The above stance is often accompanied by an arm held across the chest (Fig 6). This arm is a barrier as impenetrable as any wall. What you have to do is remove that barrier. You also have to persuade him to lean towards you.

While at the interview, you may care to pay attention to your own arm barrier signals. When people are among strangers at a cocktail party or in an elevator, for instance, the urge is invariably to fold their arms. 'Wallflowers' at dances sit with their arms folded. They want to take part, otherwise why would they be there? But they feel desperately insecure. Notice, though, that when they are approached and engaged in conversation, the arm barrier usually comes down.

The folded arms gesture signifies a negative or defensive attitude. In the negative aspect, people who feel out of their depth fold their arms. In the defensive, folded arms will signify disagreement more graphically than practically any other cue.

Some authorities suggest that the arm folded stance is an echo from the days of swords and shields. The arms now take the place of the shield, guarding the chest from an aggressor.

Arms held behind the back, on the other hand, signal

Fig 6.   The Three Stages of Evaluation.
1. **Chin stroke. Arm barrier up. Leans back.**
2. **Sits upright. Inclines head. He's coming round.**
3. **Leans forward. Drops arm barrier. He's practically convinced.**

openness and confidence — you don't have any worries about exposing your chest. You can handle anything that comes along. The male members of the Royal Family classically employ the arms-behind-the-back stance, as do many politicians and senior military personnel — the latter, most pointedly, when they are inspecting their troops.

Another demonstration of negative mood is when the hands are clenched either at waist height, or as in Fig 7, at chin height.

Were this woman to be interviewing you — beware; she is definitely not as amicable as she might be, and is quietly critical. To get her round to your point-of-view, you have to 'persuade' her to unclasp those hands.

Fig 7.   Her clasped hands demonstrate a negative mood.

Now take a look at Fig 8. On the basis of what we've learned, which of these three interviewees is making the right impression on you?

Interviewee A is sending out all the defensive signals. His arms are folded tightly, and his ankles are crossed. He is not a happy man.

Interviewee B is a little more open, yet those tightly closed fists show apprehension. Inside him, there is a fight going on for self control.

Interviewee C, on the other hand, is demonstrating openness. The open palms, the body leaning forward, the legs apart, all add up to someone who feels confident and happy.

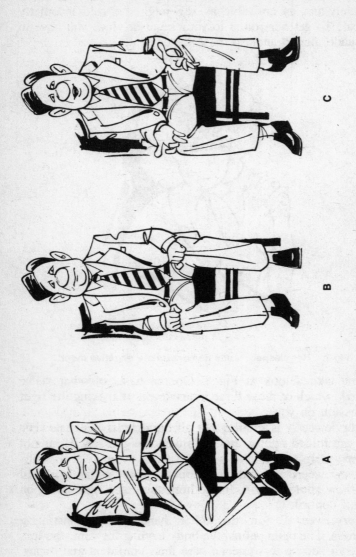

Fig 8. Who is making the best impression?

Fig 9.   Some interviewers like to demonstrate their power.
          This show of status is most noticeable in the
          layout of the interview room...

Some interviewers like to demonstrate their power. This show of strength is most noticeable in the layout of the interview room. (See Fig 9.) A massive, overblown desk, and a large, overstuffed chair are the accoutrements of the power-hungry. By contrast, the seat put aside for visitors is small, uncomfortable and, like as not, rickety. For the best possible effect, the interviewer places the visitor chair as far from his desk as space allows. Like this, the interviewee is figuratively and literally out in the cold.

An interviewee who accepts this situation deserves the rejection that he will most certainly get. But the smart punter will move his seat closer to the interviewer — not as a seemingly deliberate act, but while introducing himself, or while enthusing about his work experience. And he will do it smoothly, with panache, as though it is the most natural act in the world.

Where should he re-site the chair?

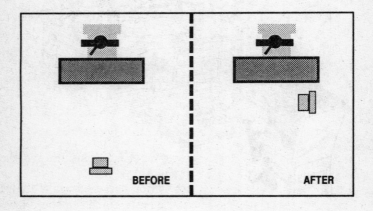

Fig 10. Try to move closer to the interviewer.

First, within the manager's Social Zone — about one-and-a-half metres from the tip of the cigar! If space allows, the chair should also be placed at a right-angle to the manager's. In this configuration, the barrier created by the desk is much reduced; and his knees will not be restricted. (See Fig 10.)

The power-crazy, fortunately, are few and far between; the remainder are simply doing what is, after all, a very difficult job. The majority, then, won't try to impress you. On the contrary, they'll expect you to impress *them*.

Many interviews are conducted quite informally, particularly so the higher up the executive rung you go. These non-ritualized meetings are often held at a boardroom table; and in such cases there is always the opportunity to choose where you

Fig 11.   The female candidate has chosen her position well.

sit in relation to the interviewer. Thus, if you are offered the chance, position yourself as in Fig 11.

Here, the lady has elected to position herself at right angles to the interviewer. It's just about the best choice she could have made, since it's more likely to promote cordiality.

Where you are unable to select your position, by far the best stance to adopt is shown in Fig 12. The upper body leans

Fig 12.   The woman appears keen and open.

slightly towards the interviewer; the hands are apart and are resting on the table — thereby allowing a palm display from time to time. The woman's cues make her appear keen and open, which etches a good impression on the manager's mind.

Incidentally, don't be alarmed or put out if the interviewer turns sideways on to you (Fig 12) and addresses you over his shoulder. He is only trying to make you feel at ease.

But back to the handshake. As the great American writer, Ralph Waldo Emerson said: 'I hate the giving of the hand unless the whole man accompanies it.' 'Nuff said.

And that, for interview purposes, is all you need to know about body language. There is, obviously, a lot more to it than I've outlined here. So should you feel inclined to go the full route, I suggest you lay hands on a book dedicated to the subject.

10.

How To Take The Strain
Out Of Letter Writing

Hands up all those who hate writing letters. Well, you are not alone. But why should this be? Why is letter writing to some people what green kryptonite is to Superman?

I'll tell you.

The great proportion of people sit down to write a letter *without having a clear idea of what they want to say.* They somehow hope that the message will resolve itself as they proceed. Mostly it doesn't; with the result that the letter is obscure, repetitious and self-conscious.

The first principle of letter writing, therefore, is to establish the Subject Elements before you start. In other words, prepare a framework outlining exactly what you want to say.

Let's see how that works.

You want to write to a local d.i.y. warehouse which has advertised for an assistant sales manager. Ideally, they need someone who is used to retail selling; but anyone with sales experience will be considered. For your part, you have nothing much to offer except a couple of years of bar-work (barman/barmaid) under your belt.

Now, your CV is prepared; but you know it probably won't be perused with much vigour unless the covering letter is powerful enough to make the personnel manager want to go farther.

So, determine the Subject Elements.

1. An opener establishing exactly which job you are applying for. (They may have advertised several.)

2. An assertion suggesting that you know what skills are required to do the job on offer.

3. A reinforcement of the above, giving the reasons why you can do it.

4. A statement outlining your motive for wanting to change jobs. (Your expectations.)

5. A mention of the enclosed CV.

6. A call to action.

In Element 1, you need to come immediately to the point. In Element 2, you require a line that will stop the reader in his tracks. The application of a little creativity is required here.

How about something like:

> Dear Mr Boat,
>
> With regard to your advertisement in the Sidmouth Clarion for an Assistant Sales Manager, I should be obliged if you would consider me for the position.

As any good barman will tell you, selling to the public is an art. It requires tact, patience and, above all, a concrete belief in one's products and services.

Followed by the reinforcement (Element 3):

As a good barman myself, with two years' service in one of the city's most popular licensed houses, I have extensive experience of dealing directly with the public. I am also familiar with stock-control and daily accounts control.

Plus Element 4:

At this stage in my career, I am anxious to widen my horizons and accept greater responsibilities. And I feel that my skills could best be developed and employed within a retail sales organisation such as yours. I am fast to learn and keen for success. Both of which attributes, I feel, could be of benefit to you.

Now for the CV (Element 5):

The enclosed Curriculum Vitae enlarges upon my career to date, and will tell you everything you need to know.

And the call to action:

Of course, I would greatly welcome the opportunity to meet you to discuss the foregoing. Accordingly, sir, I shall make myself available at any time for interview.

Yours sincerely,

What have you accomplished here? Plenty. You've exhibited a modicum of flair — a necessary attribute for any sales person. You've demonstrated how your experience, however dissimilar it is from that required for the job on offer, can be turned to good use. And you've outlined worthwhile career objectives which will probably coincide with the company's own specification for the job.

I reckon you're a racing certainty for an interview at least. However, as I said back in Chapter 7, don't look upon your first draft as final. Work on it, edit it, put it away for a day or two, then re-hash it. Like this, you'll end up with a real gem. (But watch you don't miss the closing date for applications, eh?)

Yeah, that's all very well, you may say. But what if I want to write out of the blue to a company which hasn't advertised?

To which I reply: the same principles apply. Before you do anything set out the Subject Elements. Like this, perhaps:

1. Outline your reasons for approaching this company. (Though not on the lines of: 'Oi, I need a job.')

2. Briefly state your skills or experience, and relate them to the company's type of business.

3. Establish your benefits to the company if it is wise enough to hire you.

4. Mention the enclosed CV.

5. Call to action.

When you write out these Subject Elements, of course, you will jot down the data relevant to each point. Don't try to keep it in your head, you'll probably forget something important and then have to re-draft the whole thing.

Right — in this example, we'll assume that, for one reason or another, you have only a modest academic record and have, consequently, been in a variety of unrelated and dead-end jobs. For instance, printer's labourer, double-glazing salesman, mini-cab driver. You are currently interested in anything you can get; but a job in sales would be to your taste.

We'll also speculate that the company in question is in the business of hand tool manufacturing. Imperatively, you will have done some homework on the company before writing — isn't that so?

Here we go.

Dear Mr Boat,

My researches show that your company has launched no less than three trade promotions this year. This suggests to me that production is outstripping demand, and that your product range may yet need a further boost.

I think I can help you resolve this situation. By becoming the best salesman you have ever hired.

I have sales experience. I have professional driving experience. And I am unafraid of hard work. As my enclosed CV, which I respectfully ask you to read, should graphically prove.

By popular consent, your company manufactures the finest tools anyone laid a hand on. I would like to help sustain that reputation.

If this strikes you, as it does me, as something deserving further discussion, I shall be very pleased to hear from you.

Yours sincerely,

You think this is too strong? What do you have to lose? If you want to make job applications like everyone else makes job applications, go right ahead. But if you want to stand out from the crowd, do something with guts to it and demonstrate some fire in your belly.

I'll tell you something else. For trawl letters, I should also be inclined to use a headline to attract attention and deliver an immediate message.

For someone with a background in computer work who is hoping to take a step up as programmer, a suitable headline might run:

Dear Mr Cake,

IF I CAN'T DO IT, YOU DON'T NEED IT!

(And then go on to demonstrate why.)

With trawl letters, there are no limits (decency prevailing, of course) to what you can say, just so long as your objective is to pull a response. And you don't need to be all that original either. Swipe a pertinent headline from a newspaper or magazine, re-hash it if necessary, and use it.

In the words of American columnist Sholem Asch: 'Writing comes more easily if you have something to say.' I can do no more than add: so experiment, and say something worth hearing.

Oh, you can put your hands down now.

11.

Your Handwriting Can Speak Volumes

It's a fact that the average psycho-analyst can understand a lot about his patients' psychological problems simply by asking them to relate their dreams. I'm willing to bet, however, that he can tell just as much, and possibly more, when he asks them to write a cheque to cover his fee. Because while dreams are abstract, and the thread of them may be lost in translation, the handwriting on the cheque is a material witness to the writer's inner self.

Handwriting, like speech, is a projection of your thoughts and is, therefore, a tangible indicator of your personality and character. Just as the way you dress is a statement about your mood, or the impression you wish to make upon the world, so your writing can be a very real representation of the kind of person you are.

For the purposes of getting a job, then, your handwriting may make the difference between appointment and disappointment.

It's no secret that the larger companies in the UK are more and more employing graphologists to analyse applicants' handwriting. I understand, too, that smaller companies are placing greater importance on handwriting; and while these firms may not be in a position to buy the services of a professional to vet submissions, they will certainly have formulated guidelines for judging given aspects of them. Hence the plethora of ads requesting applications in the candidate's own hand.

This chapter is the result of interviews with two writing analysts and one professional graphologist. While they displayed almost total unanimity in the general, they differed somewhat in the particular. This is to say that the basic principles of handwriting analysis seem to be universal; only the finer points are arguable. To clarify that, yet again, it all boils down to whether the analyst sees a particular feature in a piece of writing as having a positive or negative characteristic.

For example, the use of strong pressure on the paper, indicated by very broad strokes, if taken negatively, might suggest that the writer is over-forceful and domineering. Conversely, from a positive standpoint, it could intimate strength of character and power of thought.

This is why, logically enough, analysts never view a single characteristic in isolation. They will, invariably, assess all the clues of legibility, regular rhythm, consistency, angle, height, depth, speed, artistry, and so on, before arriving at a positive or negative conclusion.

It is, as you may now judge, a vast and complex subject which could fill an entire library of books. For this reason, I shall confine myself to the basic principles of handwriting analysis, highlighting those danger areas quickly picked up and leaped upon by analysts. There should, however, be enough here to help you transmit the right signals when you make your next hand-written application.

We shall begin with your signature. When you write your name at the end of a letter, try to make sure that it is no larger and, indeed, no smaller than the name of your addressee. The example, here, clearly shows that the writer feels himself more significant than the recipient. Not a good start.

Dear Mr Cake,
(blah, blah, blah)

Yours sincerely,
Roland Butter.

Signature larger than the addressee's name.

A legible signature or an illegible one, that is the question? An illegible signature can indicate that the writer is more concerned with the content of his letter than he is with himself. For this reason, 'business' signatures are often unreadable, but the writers of these will pen a perfectly good version when they are on intimate terms with the reader. On the other hand, it could show a marked lack of self esteem.

The underlined signature graphically draws attention to the writer's name. Pay attention to this, it says, I am important. While the signature partially obscured by a line displays a certain self-negation and even a self-destructive tendency. He is, in effect, crossing himself out!

Rita Brown.

Joseph Smith

Robert Green

Top: Underlined for attention.
Centre: Self-critically crossed out.
Bottom: Enlarged capitals denote a desire for
formality and tradition.

Overlarge capital letters are indicative of the writer's regard for traditional values and formality. He's a small 'c' conservative. On the other hand, signature capitals that are smaller than the capitals in the rest of a letter's text show completely the reverse – the writer is informal and welcomes change.

Unquestionably, there are as many sizes of writing as there are styles, so gauging size is a relative exercise. Nonetheless, there is much to be said, and much to be learned, in respect of handwriting size.

For instance, tiny writing is indicative of people who tend to be self-sufficient and self-reliant, and who are modest about their achievements. Sometimes, the originator of very small writing may be diagnosed as being a bit of a recluse who might be difficult to incorporate into a team.

The author of very large writing is quite the opposite. He or she craves attention and might be prone to boastfulness. On the plus side, such a personality would certainly lead from the front — given that they had leadership qualities.

What about writing that contains a jumble of both small and large letters — where, for instance, a lower-case 'a' in one word is small, and in another much bigger? Here you have a moody character; someone who cannot be consistent and who is somewhat childish in attitude.

Yet even in rigidly regular, neither large nor small, writing, where uniformity is the order of the day, there can be a negative characteristic. Someone this self-disciplined might be too keen to 'go by the book' and be excessively conformist. Even so, it can also demonstrate a tidy mind. (Thus, a sales promotions firm recruiting an 'ideas man' might shy away from such evidence, while a solicitor's office looking for a general manager would leap at it.)

As we discovered in the chapter on body language, the act of leaning forward is a sign of interest and an indication of 'let's get on with it'. The same applies to the forward slant (slanting to the right) in handwriting. The author is anxious to get his thoughts down before he forgets them. On the negative side, when considered with other factors, the forward slant could also be a sign of congenital impatience.

The backward (left) slanting writer is a dog of another breed, because what he is doing is a contradiction. Where the process of writing is a progression from the left of the page to the right, why does he fight against it and go back over ground already covered? Is he a driver with a foot permanently on the brake? Is he afraid of going too far too fast?

Just like the interviewer who leans back in his chair, or retreats from us, as we are talking, the backward slanting writer is probably displaying a negative attitude.

I should point out that there are, literally, degrees of right and left slope. Extreme right slant is the work of someone who does nothing by halves, he's a real extremist; while extreme left slant tells us that the author is locked into his past and is, for the most part, emotionally unapproachable.

You might as well know it: I can't write in a straight line to save my life. Some people seem to be able to go from one margin to another without so much as a millimetre's fluctuation. Others, like me, are all over the shop. The simple answer is to rule some guide lines, but to write business letters on lined paper would be to display our immaturity and would doubtless elicit the thumbs down we rightly deserve. So I guess we'll have to try harder.

1. _Erratic rising and falling like this._

2. _Rising from the baseline._

3. _Diving towards the bottom._

4. _Rising at first, then falling_

5. _Some words jump up, or drop down._

In the meantime, take a look at how writing that's anything less than perfectly horizontal can be interpreted.

To get this into perspective, we'll need to draw an imaginary baseline on which to sit our efforts; and it's from this baseline that we measure the fluctuation. I think it goes without saying that writing which sticks to this baseline like two strips of Velcro, displays the writer's total self-control and his amazingly high level of personal discipline.

In No. 1, we have a character who is, to put it bluntly, a little unstable. If this erratic tendency appears only intermittently, then he's suffering some kind of stress; but if it's a permanent feature of his writing, he is emotionally spaced out!

In No. 2, the ascending script depicts a writer with rising ambitions. He may have a cock-eye for straightness, but he really wants to go places.

Example 3 is the work of a tired or dispirited man. He doesn't have the energy or the inclination to attempt to keep the line straight.

Line No. 4 speaks volumes about losing interest half way through a task. This fellow begins every job with a burst of enthusiasm, but soon wearies of it.

In No. 5, you can see that he likes the word 'jump', yet dislikes 'down'. Handwriting that has individual words (or phrases) above or below the general flow indicates the writer's enthusiasm for the former and a coolness for the latter.

We now come to the analysis of spacing between words and lines:

Wide spacing between words:

Is a sure sign that the writer is a bit of a loner. He or she does not, as a habit, indulge in close relationships.

But minimal spacing between words:

Means quite the opposite. Our friend has a craving for friendship and applause. It could also mean that he or she is a mite selfish.

Extremely wide spacing between lines,

just like wide word spacing:

Shows someone who has learned from experience that people can let you down. So he tends to keep them at arm's length.

On the other hand, lines tightly packed,
something like this example:

Tell us that the writer can't get the words down quickly enough. His hand won't keep up with his brain. His eagerness may lead to slipshod work and decisions.

While variable spacing between the lines,

some wide and some narrow, along
the lines of this example:

Are representative of someone who blows hot and cold on relationships. One day he gives you the big 'hello!'; next day he cuts you dead.

When a trained graphologist comes to consider a piece of writing, the first thing he does is divide the lines into zones, thus:

Example of divided zones

UPPER
MIDDLE
LOWER

The handwriting is now considered in relation to these three zones which, for our purposes can be related like this: the upper zone represents your head; the middle zone your body; and the lower zone your legs and feet.

All right. Where a person's handwriting shows all three zones to be consistently balanced (as in the above example), they are then judged to be consistent types; level-headed and with their feet firmly on the ground.

UPPER
MIDDLE
LOWER

Now look at this stylised letter 'p' with its descending tail reaching down beyond the lower zone. What do we read into this? Well, this writer works on instinct rather than logic. This is the fellow who says: 'I'm going to trust my gut feeling.'

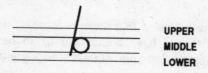

UPPER
MIDDLE
LOWER

So what about the long ascender on the above stylised letter 'b'? It tells us that the writer has his head above the crowd. He is intelligent and very, very ambitious.

Meanwhile, the dominant middle zone of this 'b' suggests someone who is self-reliant and, often, self-centred. Such people like to lead, rather than be led.

Finally, the understated middle zone in the word 'pool' is indicative of the deep thinker who is not keen on the limelight, and who is happy to put the good of the community before himself.

The foregoing is all very simple stuff, indeed; and these examples are across-the-board generalizations. But they are, nonetheless, generally true.

You could, I suppose, drive yourself halfway round the bend worrying about whether you have shown psychotic, or worse, dipsomaniac tendencies in your latest letter of application. Then again, if your writing is as scruffy and as inconsistent as mine is, it may be well worth taking a little extra care with your next application.

You may have gathered that there is more — much more — to graphology than I have committed us to here. So, once again, I recommend that you lay hands on a good book on the subject.

Despite this, I think we have learned enough to keep the analysts guessing when our next letter tips up before them.

Agreed?

Appendix

Back in the Interview Techniques chapter, I reproduced a candidate assessment chart used by personnel managers. I think it might be a good idea to give you another, slightly varied version, which is employed by a number of large companies.

To use it, ask someone close to you (someone who knows you well, but who is not afraid to be critical), to mark it up with points out of ten for each item. Allow them to do it alone and unhindered. The higher your score, the better prospects you will have of coming through an interview unscathed. It will also help you to bone up on any weak areas since, doubtless, you will quiz whoever is helping you about why they awarded high points in one area and low in another.

The 'possible' is 190 points − if you reach it, you are truly a prince (or a princess) among men (or women); and I will take leave to doubt you! Anything over 100 and you have excellent prospects; 95 is average; while 50 and below means that you have to go back and read this book over again.

But whatever you do, please don't fall out over it. It's not *that* serious.

JOB PROFILING TEST

	POINTS out of 10
AMBITIOUS FOR SUCCESS	
CONFIDENT WITH PEOPLE	
SHARES DECISIONS	
WANTS TO WIN AT ALL COSTS	
CAN BE PERSUASIVE/SELLS IDEAS	
SYMPATHETIC & TOLERANT	
CONCERNED WITH DETAILS	
LIKES TEAMWORK	
AVOIDS TALKING ABOUT SELF	
USES SOLID FACTS IN ARGUMENT	
FEELINGS ARE DIFFICULT TO HURT	
LIKES VARIETY IN WORK	
ALWAYS SEES A JOB THROUGH	
CAN SWITCH OFF FROM WORK	
IS CONSIDERED A LEADER	
GENERATES CREATIVE IDEAS	
LOGICAL PROBLEM SOLVER	
IS OPTIMISTIC	
ENJOYS PHYSICAL EXERCISE	
TOTAL	

THE RIGHT WAY TO SPELL

A high proportion of professional people are plagued by an inability to spell many common words. However, with the help of this book anyone can learn the rules of spelling and how words are built up. The book teaches the logic of English spelling (whilst not ignoring its idiosyncrasies!), explains its basis and how it has evolved over centuries. It is easily readable and memorable, yet can also be used as a quick reference guide in moments of doubt.

THE RIGHT WAY TO WRITE YOUR OWN CV

Make sure your CV *stands out* and gets noticed so that you are invited for that all-important interview! The author, John Clarke, is one of the UK's foremost professional CV compilers and has written hundreds of CVs for people seeking every imaginable kind of employment.

THE RIGHT WAY TO IMPROVE YOUR ENGLISH

Not a dull, grammar book, but an elegant exposé of the errors which people so easily make, and explanation of how these arise.

RIGHT WAY
PUBLISHING POLICY

HOW WE SELECT TITLES

RIGHT WAY consider carefully every deserving manuscript. Where an author is an authority on his subject but an inexperienced writer, we provide first-class editorial help. The standards we set make sure that every **RIGHT WAY** book is practical, easy to understand, concise, informative and delightful to read. Our specialist artists are skilled at creating simple illustrations which augment the text wherever necessary.

CONSISTENT QUALITY

At every reprint our books are updated where appropriate, giving our authors the opportunity to include new information.

FAST DELIVERY

We sell **RIGHT WAY** books to the best bookshops throughout the world. It may be that your bookseller has run out of stock of a particular title. If so, he can order more from us at any time — we have a fine reputation for "same day" despatch, and we supply any order, however small (even a single copy), to any bookseller who has an account with us. We prefer you to buy from your bookseller, as this reminds him of the strong underlying public demand for **RIGHT WAY** books. Readers who live in remote places, or who are housebound, or whose local bookseller is unco-operative, can order direct from us by post.

FREE

If you would like an up-to-date list of all **RIGHT WAY** titles currently available, please send a stamped self-addressed envelope to

ELLIOT RIGHT WAY BOOKS, KINGSWOOD, SURREY, KT20 6TD, U.K.